Power, Politics, [illegible] *Crime*

CRIME & SOCIETY

Series Editor John Hagan

University of Toronto

Betrayal and Treason: Violations of Trust and Loyalty, Nachman Ben-Yehuda

Breaking Away from Broken Windows: Baltimore Evidence and the Nationwide Fight Against Crime, Grime, Fear, and Decline, Ralph B. Taylor

Costs and Benefits of Preventing Crime, Brandon C. Welsh, David P. Farrington, and Lawrence W. Sherman

Losing Legitimacy: Street Crime and the Decline of Social Institutions in America, Gary LaFree

Public Opinion, Crime, and Criminal Justice, Julian V. Roberts and Loretta Stalans

Power, Politics and Crime, William J. Chambliss

The Community Justice Ideal, Todd Clear and David Karp

Whistleblowing at Work: Tough Choices in Exposing Fraud, Waste, and Abuse on the Job, Terance D. Miethe

Casualties of Community Disorder: Women's Careers in Violent Crime, Deborah R. Baskin and Ira B. Sommers

Poverty, Ethnicity, and Violent Crime, James F. Short

Great Pretenders: Pursuits and Careers of Persistent Thieves, Neal Shover

Crime and Public Policy: Putting Theory to Work, edited by Hugh D. Barlow

Control Balance: Toward a General Theory of Deviance, Charles R. Tittle

Rape and Society: Readings on the Problems of Sexual Assault, edited by Patricia Searles and Ronald J. Berger

Inequality, Crime, and Social Control, George S. Bridges and Martha A. Myers

FORTHCOMING

Latino Homicide: A Five-City Study, Ramiro Martinez

Power, Politics, and Crime

William J. Chambliss

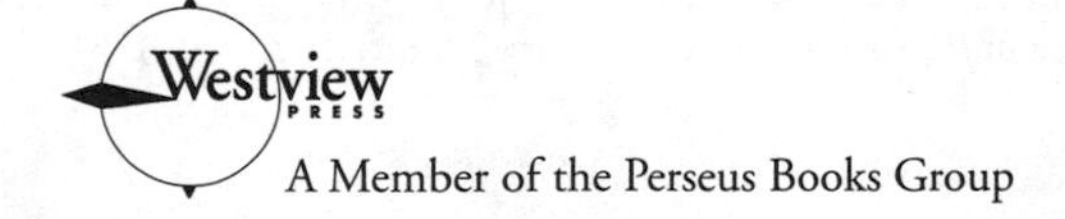

A Member of the Perseus Books Group

Crime and Society

Published in 2001 in the United States of America by Westview Press, 5500 Central Avenue, Boulder, Colorado 80301-2877, and in the United Kingdom by Westview Press, 12 Hid's Copse Road, Cumnor Hill, Oxford, OX2 9JJ

Library of Congress Cataloging-in-Publication Data
Chambliss, William J.
Power, politics, and crime / William J. Chambliss.
p. cm.—(Crime & society)
Includes bibliographical references and index.
ISBN 0-8133-3486-1 (hc) / ISBN 0-8133-3487-X (pb)
1. Crime—Political aspects—United States. 2. Criminal justice, Administration of—Political aspects—United States. I. Title.
II. Series: Crime & society (Boulder, Colo.)
HV6789.C395 1999
364.973—dc21 99-32625
CIP

The paper used in this publication meets the requirements of the American National Standard for Permanence of Paper for Printed Library Materials Z39.48-1984

10 9 8 7 6 5 4 3 2 1

For my friends and grandchildren:
Neil, Cecelia, Timmy, and John William

Contents

PART 2: PRACTICE

PART 3: IMPLICATIONS

Tables and Illustrations

Tables

Figures

Preface

Between the idea
And the reality
Between the motion
And the act
Falls the Shadow
—*T. S. Eliot*

The idea that underpins American criminal law is as noble as any ever conceived. A group of citizens are elected by their peers to enact legislation. Impartial judges uninfluenced by political considerations interpret the statutes in the light of a Constitution that guarantees every person freedom from tyranny. Police tied closely to the community work with the people to see that life is safe and peaceful for all its members.

The reality of law could not be more distant from this ideal. Legislators pass laws that most people do not know about and if they did would not understand. Judges are political appointees whose careers depend on making decisions that are compatible with the ideological prejudices of the elected officials who control their appointments. Police and prosecutors work in a bureaucracy that more often than not pits them against the people they are supposed to protect.

Police, prison guards, and people who work in what the Norwegian criminologist Nils Christie calls "the crime control industry" champion legislation to spend more tax money to ensure their employment.

The result of this process is that Americans are being scared to death about crime. In a circle with no end, we are fed distorted and misleading information and then told that the only solution to the problem (which has been manufactured by government officials in the first place) is to spend more money on policies that contribute to the problem.

We are becoming a country obsessed with an imaginary plague, spending scarce resources on failed remedies while refusing to recognize both the reality of the problem and the social policies that do work. We must bring about a revolution in our thinking lest, too late, we realize that our fears generated policies that created the plague we feared.

It is the law enforcement bureaucracy, the politicians, the media, and the industries that profit from the building of prisons and the creation and manufacture of crime control technologies that perpetuate the myths that justify wasting vast sums of taxpayer's money on failed efforts at crime control.

This book is a study of the reality of crime in America, of how the perception of crime is manipulated by vested interests, and of the consequences for the nation of this hiatus "between the idea and the reality."

William J. Chambliss

Acknowledgments

So many people generously contributed their time, knowledge, insight, and effort to make this book possible that it would take almost another whole book to thank them: First and foremost, I am indebted to Ed Sbarbaro and Justin Baer, who coauthored Chapters 1 and 2. I am equally indebted to the police whom I accompanied on their patrols; the people in the ghettos who talked with me; the adolescents who let me follow their antics and who talked at length about their lives; the drug dealers, gamblers, professional thieves, and politicians who over the years provided insights and firsthand experience that form the basis of generalizations. I have benefited greatly from and used in the manuscript information and ideas provided by the Lindesmith Center of the Soros Foundation and the dedicated people who work for UNION (United for No Injustice, Oppression, or Neglect). Barbara Cayenne Bird, executive director of UNION, works tirelessly to keep all of us abreast of news reports and other relevant information. To her I owe a very special thanks.

I am also indebted to the students who worked with me on research projects for their intellectual stimulation and keen observations that formed the basis for the various chapters: Jeffrey Rickert, Shari Kagan, Eliassa Greenberg, Barry Holman, Phil Beatty, and Jon Anderson spent many tedious hours gathering data and many exciting hours discussing ideas that contributed to the making of the final product. In the final stages of preparation Joe McCahill, Carol Fugita, and Shannon Weiss checked and updated data, tables, and graphs long into the night. I owe them a very special thanks. John Galliher, Martha Huggins, and Mark Hamm read the manuscript, made invaluable suggestions, and encouraged me to carry on with the project. Finally, I am very grateful to two dear journalistic friends who provided invaluable editorial assistance: Julie Bowles Makinen of the *Washington Post*, and the Washington, D.C., financial correspondent for the *Evening Standard,* who happens also to be my daughter, Lauren Chambliss.

As always, I am forever grateful to my wife, Pernille, for her patience, support, and critical inquisitiveness, which forced me to dig deep for data to support my theories and sharpen the arguments.

Whatever shortcomings remain are those they could do nothing about.

W. J. C.

Introduction: Misperceptions of Crime

The facts are simple enough: For the last twenty-five years the crime rate in the United States has been steadily declining. Most people, however, believe that the United States is a sea of aggression in which their lives and their property are subject to whimsical violence and attack by predators. Consequently, federal, state, and local governments ceaselessly increase expenditures on crime control while at the same time cutting back in practically every other area.

The federal budget for crime control tripled from $1,077 billion in 1995 to an estimated $4,541 billion in 1999.[1] The number of federal law enforcement officers increased 11 percent, with Immigration and Naturalization Services increasing a whopping 34 percent. During the 1990s entire bureaus of federal and state governments were eliminated in an effort to save money and scale back "big government." Congress passed and President Bill Clinton signed a welfare bill that reduced federal spending on welfare by $60 billion. Spending was cut for Medicare, Social Security, and a host of public services, including the Post Office and public transportation, to reduce federal and state budget deficits. Even expenditures on the once sacrosanct military were reduced. But the budgets for policing and prisons grew like Topsy, increasing every year at all levels of government.

While government agencies and private citizens scramble to survive with less, the criminal justice system—police, prosecutors, courts, and prisons—search for ways to spend the largesse created by dramatic increases in government funding. For example, in 1994 Congress passed and President Clinton signed into law a bill authorizing the expenditure of nearly $24 billion to enable state and municipal governments to hire 100,000 new police officers and to construct new prisons. In 1998 federal funds were made available for selected cities to hire 700 more police officers. The federal budget for the so-called War on Drugs rose from $1 billion in 1980 to nearly $20 billion in 2000. The number of people in prison and jails quadrupled between 1980 and 2000, necessitating a huge increase in public expenditures for building prisons and incarcerating inmates. Currently over 170,000 new prison beds are being constructed at a cost of $8.5 billion. The cost of incarcerating inmates adds an additional $30 billion a year.[2]

That the United States has a crime problem cannot be denied, but the problem is not nearly as serious as people have been led to believe. The solutions being pursued do more to exacerbate the problem than to solve it. The crime problem in the United States is neither better nor worse today than it was fifty years ago, when people were not afraid to walk the streets at night or to leave their car unlocked in their driveway. The *perception* of the American people has changed; the severity of the problem has not. The rate of both violent and nonviolent crime has actually declined in the past twenty-five years. (See Figure I.1.) Americans are probably as safe today as they have ever been.

Every year for the past twenty-five years the Bureau of the census interviews a sample of more than 100,000 citizens and asks whether they have been the victim of any kind of crime, including minor incidents of theft, assault, or harassment. The results of these surveys show that in any given year almost 90 percent of Americans are not the victims of *any* criminal offense. The risk of being a victim of a violent crime is even less: In any given year fewer than 3 percent of Americans are victims of a violent crime. Every year 50,000 people die and hundreds of thousands are injured in automobile accidents. There are fewer than 20,000 homicides every year, and violent crime does not approach automobile accidents for the number of injuries caused. Indeed, what the FBI calls "violent crimes," such as robbery, rarely result in the hospitalization of the victim, whereas automobile accidents are much more likely to require hospitalization.

People most fear being victimized by a stranger. But violent crimes are more likely to be committed by a relative or close friend of the victim than by a stranger. You are much more likely to be the victim of a violent crime in your own home than you are on the streets.

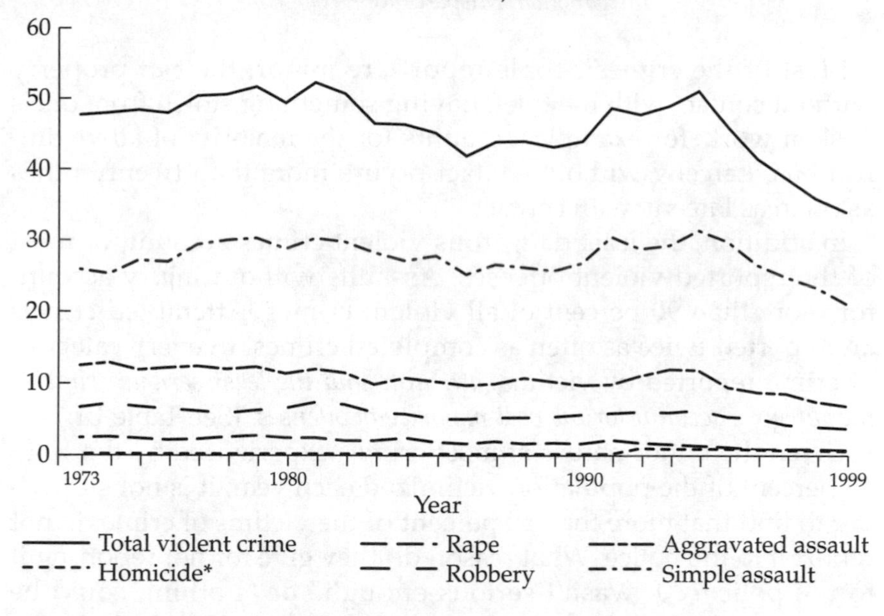

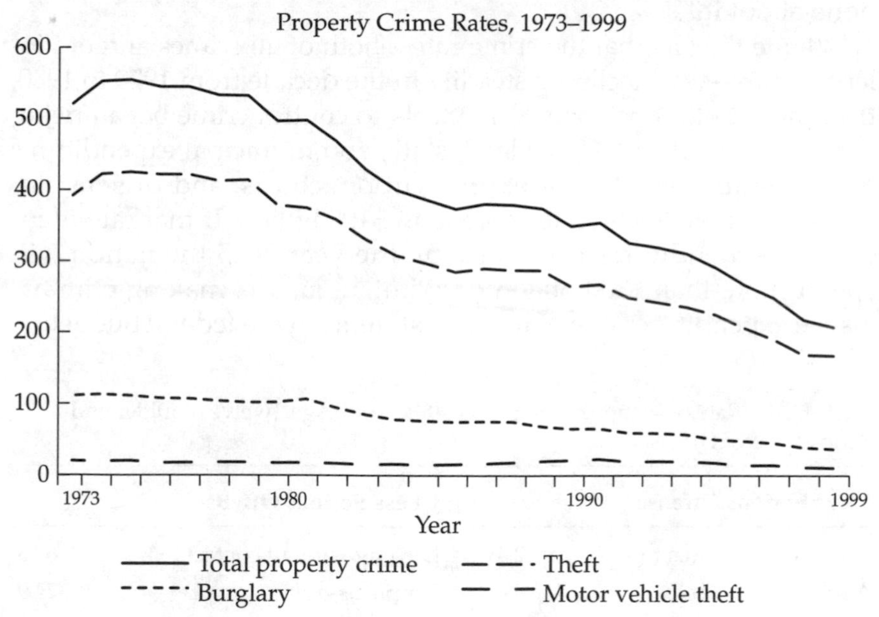

FIGURE I.1 Violent and Property Crime Rates, 1973–1999

SOURCE: Bureau of Justice Statistics, "Criminal Victimization, 1973–1999" (Washington, D.C.: U.S. Department of Justice, 1973–1999, Federal Bureau of Investigation, *Uniform Crime Reports*, 1973–1999.

*NOTE: Homicide data are from the *Uniform Crime Reports*; all other data are from National Criminal Victim Surveys.

Most of the crimes people report are minor: theft of property without contact with the thief; having something stolen from one's desk at work, for example, accounts for the majority of all victimizations. Larceny without contact occurs more than twenty times as often as larceny with contact.

In addition, the least dangerous violent crimes account for most of the reported violent offenses: Assaults without injury account for more than 90 percent of all violent crimes. Attempted crimes are reported twice as often as completed crimes. In every category of crime reported by victims, *attempts and the least serious crime in the category account for the vast majority of offenses.* (See Table I.1.)

Given the minor nature of most crimes experienced by the 10 to 15 percent of the population victimized each year, it is not surprising to find that more than 50 percent of the victims of crime do not report it to the police. What reason do they give for not reporting it to the police? "It wasn't serious enough" or "nothing could be done about it."[3]

Despite the fact that the crime rate—both of all crimes and of violent crimes—was declining steadily in the decade from 1970 to 1980, the amount of money spent on efforts to control crime began rising exponentially after 1982. Federal, state, and municipal expenditures on law enforcement (police, prosecution, courts, and prisons) increased from $36 billion to more than $100 billion. If that rate of increased expenditures continues, by the year 2005 the nation will spend more than $200 billion on criminal justice, making criminal justice expenditures one of the largest items in the federal budget.

TABLE I.1 Rate of Victimization per 1,000 Persons Age Twelve or Older and Seriousness of Offense

More Serious Offense		Less Serious Offense	
Larceny with contact	2.4	Larceny without contact	60.6
Aggravated assault	8.6	Simple assault	24.9
Aggravated assault with injury	2.7	Aggravated assault without injury	5.9
Robbery with injury	1.1	Robbery without injury	2.3
Attempted robbery with injury	0.3	Attempted robbery without injury	1.2
Completed crmes of violence	12.2	Attempted crimes of violence	27.0
Completed rapes	0.4	Atempted rapes	0.5

The Rising American Prison Population

The percentage of the U.S. population in prison has risen steadily since the 1930s, and in recent years the increase has been dramatic. Between 1980 and 2000 the number of people under the control of the criminal justice system (in prison, in jail, and on probation or parole) rose from fewer than 2 million to more than 6 million, a threefold increase in less than twenty years. The number of people in prison grew even faster, by nearly 300 percent from fewer than 320,000 inmates in 1980 to nearly 2 million in 2000. (See Figure I.2.)

The year 1995 marked a watershed for the United States: For the first time in our history, we had a higher percentage of our population in prison or jail than any other Western industrialized country. (See Figure I.3.) The United States incarcerates ten times as many people as Japan and more than five times as many as Italy, France, Great Britain, Spain, or Australia.[4]

The Growing Prison Economy

Between 1982 and 2000 the number of people employed in the criminal justice system increased by nearly 50 percent. The number of full-time federal criminal justice employees grew from 95,000 in 1982 to more than 170,000 in 2000. Crime control, prison construction, and maintaining people in prison and jails have become one of the nation's major growth industries.

Who is filling our jails and prisons? Most of the victims of the criminal justice system are minor offenders. According to a study conducted by the National Center for Crime and Delinquency, more than 50 percent of the prisoners in state and federal prisons are there for offenses that, according to public opinion surveys, the general public thinks are "not very serious crimes." (See Figure I.4.)[5]

More than 60 percent of all inmates of federal prisons were sentenced for drug offenses. A study conducted at the request of the attorney general, which was not made public, found that more than 30 percent of the federal prisoners sentenced for drug offenses *had no history of violent crime or other felonies, and were not engaged in any ongoing criminal enterprises, such as the sale or manufacture of drugs.* These prisoners are drug addicts, not drug dealers.

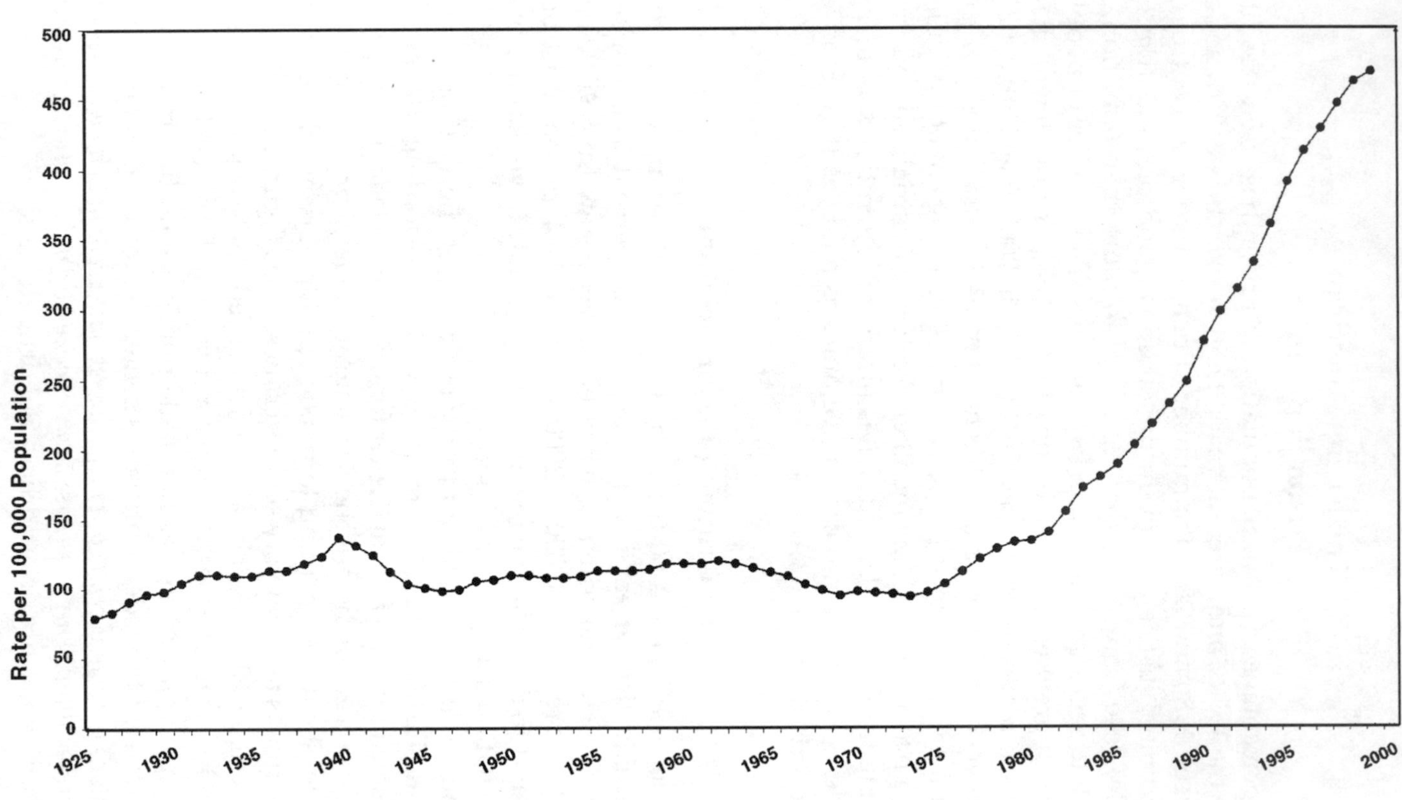

FIGURE I.2 Sentenced Prisoners in State and Federal Institutions, 1925–2000

SOURCE: U.S. Department of Justice, Bureau of Criminal Justice Statistics, Washington, D.C.

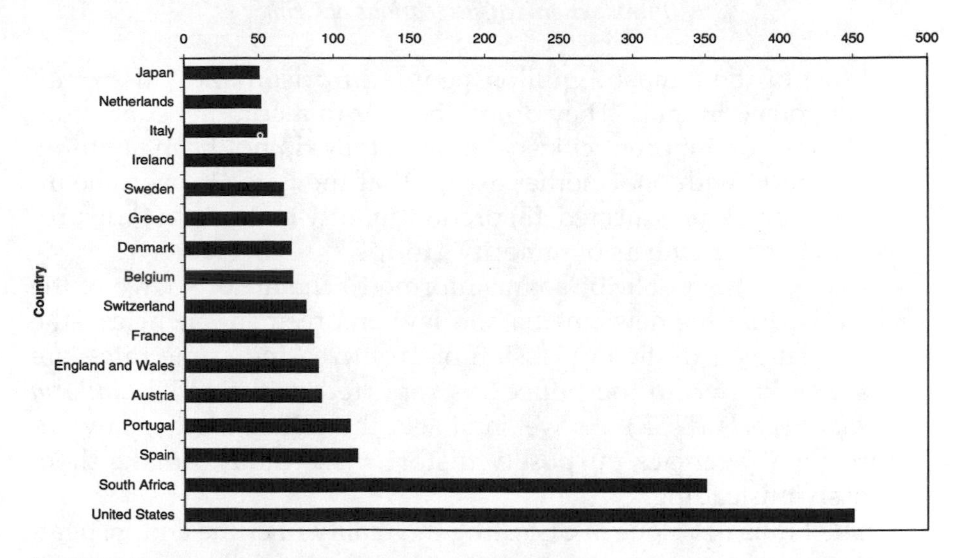

FIGURE I.3 International Incarceration Rates, 1992

SOURCE I.4: Annie Kensy and Pierre Tournier, *French Prison Population: some features,* (Paris: Direction de l'administration penitentiaire, Ministrie de la Justice, 1997), 2.

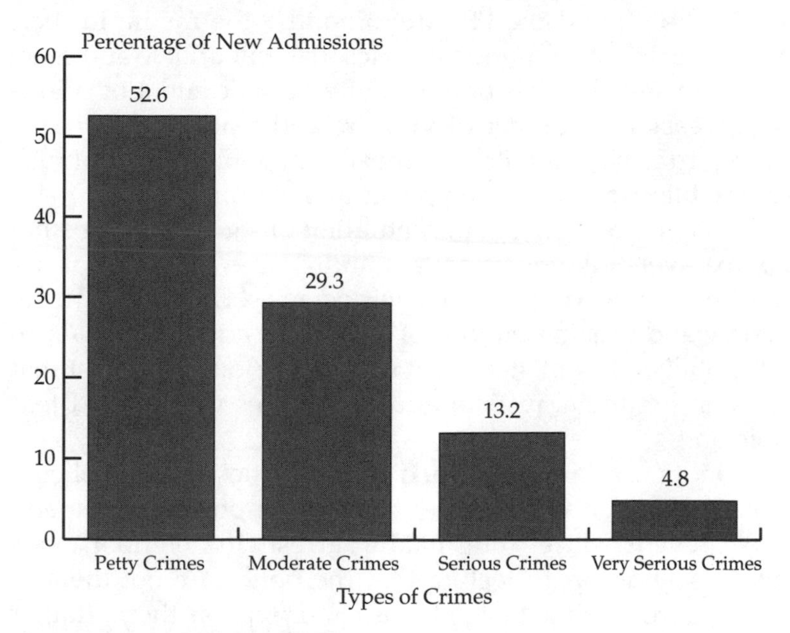

FIGURE I.4 Public Estimation of the Severity of Crimes Committed by Persons Incarcerated in Federal and State Prisons

SOURCE: James Austin and John Irwin, *Who Goes to Prison?* (San Francisco: National Council on Crime and Delinquency, 1987).

Most of the almost 2 million people in prison and jail are not dangerous criminals. They do not belong to a criminal subculture that preys on innocent citizens. In fact, they do not have anything in common with one another except that they are (1) overwhelmingly poor, (2) uneducated, (3) predominantly male, and (4) disproportionately members of minority groups.

How can the public be so misinformed? The major source of the data used by the news media and law enforcement agencies—the data that lead to the impression of an increasing crime rate—are "crimes known to the police" as reported in the FBI's *Uniform Crime Reports* (*UCR*). As we shall see, the FBI and other law enforcement agencies purposely distort these data to make them grossly misleading.

The FBI is not alone in distorting the reality of crime and instigating panics. Local law enforcement agencies gleefully reinforce FBI statistics by seeking publicity for sensational crimes and by manufacturing "crime waves." Local police are very effective at creating panics over particular types of crime, such as carjackings and gang warfare. The police and the FBI are joined by the media in their never-ending search for sensational topics that will titillate and exacerbate the fears and anxieties of the viewing public and, not coincidentally, increase the number of viewers and readers. Politicians desperate for an issue guaranteed to meet with public approval rush to increase public expenditures on police and prisons.

The result is the creation and perpetuation of a gigantic hoax that costs the taxpayers billions of dollars and creates a system of oppression unprecedented in modern democracies. Distorting the reality of crime and wasting billions of dollars on crime control is an egregious public policy mistake. But equally serious is the fact that the burgeoning criminal justice industry creates widespread fear and suspicion.

In the economically impoverished communities where policing is most intense, anger and hostility toward the police is rampant. Onlookers prevent police from making arrests in neighborhoods where there is widespread feeling that the police are not there to protect people from crime but to harass and oppress them. Rather than promoting a sense of security among residents in the neighborhoods where crime rates are highest, policing increases the division between the black and white populations by reinforcing the white community's perception of young black men as dangerous and criminal and by reinforcing the black community's perception of the police as a hostile, occupying army.

There is, in short, a huge chasm between the reality of crime, the public's perception of it, and the information being disseminated to the public by law enforcement agencies, the media, and politicians.

How this discrepancy between the reality of crime, the public's perception, and government expenditures has come to pass and its consequences for the quality of life in the United States is the subject of this book. In Part I, I examine the role of politics and law enforcement in the creation of the "crime problem." In Part II, I look at the criminal law in action: how the day-to-day decisions of law enforcement agencies affect the perception of crime and criminality in America. Finally, in Part III, I take up the issue of what effect the political, law enforcement, and media practices have on U.S. society and what can be done to change current policies and practices.

Notes

1. Executive Office of the President, *Budget of the United States Government: Historical Tables* (Washington, D.C.: GPO, 1998).
2. James Austin, "National Policy Statement," presented to the American Society of Criminology, Institute on Crime, Justice, and Corrections, Washington, D.C., March 2000.
3. Bureau of Justice Statistics. *Criminal Victimization in the United States* (Washington, D.C.: U.S. Department of Justice, 1988).
4. Nils Christie, *Crime Control as Industry* (London: Routledge, 1997), 29.
5. James Austin and John Irwin. *Who Goes to Prison?* (San Francisco: National Council on Crime and Delinquency, 1987).

Part 1

Propaganda

Chapter One

The Politics of Fear

Political conservatives took a serious beating in the 1960s. The mood of the country was decidedly liberal. University campuses were in a state of virtual revolution, Marxism and other radical theories enjoyed a resurgence unknown since the depression, the Civil Rights movement mobilized millions of people demanding fundamental changes, and large sectors of the intelligentsia joined college students in actively opposing the Vietnam War.

In addition the Supreme Court overturned years of conservative criminal justice policies. The *Miranda* decision gave suspects the right to remain silent when questioned by the police, *Gideon* gave indigent defendants the right to a lawyer, and *Escobedo* limited the admissibility of defendant's statements to the police if the defendant's request to have a lawyer present had been denied.

Conservatives, however, were not without the resources to mount a counteroffensive. A cabal of leading industrialists, along with the right-wing journalist William F. Buckley, met to develop strategies to turn the tide. Wealthy Americans contributed funds to create "think tanks" that promulgated the conservative ideology, and the power elite formed political action committees (PACs) that infused massive sums into the political campaigns of conservatives.

One result of conservative mobilization against liberalism was the selection of Barry Goldwater, the darling of the conservatives, as the Republican presidential nominee in 1964.

Goldwater, whose campaign manager Holmes Alexander was an outspoken racist, ran against the Civil Rights movement, intending to break the Democratic party's traditional hold on the southern states. He advocated legislation to turn back the Civil Rights movement, which he alleged was "Communist inspired." He also sought to overturn the Supreme Court decisions enhancing the rights of criminal defendants. His focus on crime was a smoke screen for a covertly racist campaign.

Goldwater sounded the alarm in his acceptance speech at the Republican Convention: "Tonight there is violence in our streets, corruption in our highest offices, aimlessness among our youth, anxiety among our elderly . . . security from domestic violence, no less than from foreign aggression, is the most elementary and fundamental purpose of any government."[1]

On the campaign trail Goldwater hammered away at crime and used racist allusions to equate crime with African Americans and the Civil Rights movement. He placed the blame for civil disorder squarely on the shoulders of "liberals," civil rights demonstrators, and Democratic party policies that coddled criminals :

> Our wives, all women, feel unsafe on our streets. And in encouragement of even more abuse of the law, we have the appalling spectacle of this country's Ambassador to the United Nations [Adlai Stevenson] actually telling an audience—this year, at Colby College—that, "in the great struggle to advance human civil rights, even a jail sentence is no longer a dishonor but a proud achievement." Perhaps we are destined to see in this law-loving land people running for office not on their stainless records but on their prison record.[2]

Goldwater referred to civil rights as a threat to the safety of "our wives" time and again throughout the campaign. It was the most blatant attempt to link crime and violence to African Americans since the Dixiecrats (a third party of southern conservatives) opposed the Democratic civil rights stand in the 1948 presidential election.

Throughout the campaign the Democratic presidential candidate, Lyndon Johnson, argued that crime was part of the larger issue of social justice, which would be handled by his "Great Society" programs:

> Asked about the Federal Government's role in checking "crime in the streets," President Johnson said his anti-poverty program would be of "some help" and "our increased educational measures will be of

> great help. Johnson said other measures to improve "shameful" living conditions and promote the education, training, and recreation of city residents should be developed.[3]

The voters were not receptive to Goldwater's message. Less than three weeks before the election *Newsweek*'s editors wrote, "Remarkably late in the campaign, Barry Goldwater was still a candidate in search of an issue that could score a voting breakthrough . . . [He] did all he could to press the issue of law and order."[4] Johnson was reelected to the presidency by a landslide. He received the largest share of the popular vote so far recorded in the United States. He won a majority in every region of the country.[5] Clearly Goldwater's hue and cry over the danger of crime did not strike a resonant chord among the American public.

Crime never appeared in public opinion polls taken during the campaign of 1963 and 1964 as a major problem. In polls taken after the election, in May 1965, the most important problems facing the nation were said to be (in rank order) the Vietnam War, civil rights, the threat of war, prestige abroad, spread of world communism, the Dominican Republic crisis, the high cost of living, and unemployment. Only 2 percent of the respondents mentioned juvenile delinquency as the most important problem. These results were consistent with findings from polls for the preceding thirty-five years: In Gallup polls taken every year since the 1930s respondents consistently said that the most important problems facing America were unemployment, keeping out of war, the high cost of living, and inflation. In the 1950s America saw communism as a major problem, and in the 1960s they were concerned with civil rights, the Vietnam War, and race relations. (See Table 1.1) Crime was almost never mentioned, and never was it near the top of the list of most important problems. Goldwater and his strategists misidentified the issues that most concerned Americans.

Johnson had campaigned on a platform to create the Great Society, where poverty would be eliminated and everyone would have an "equal opportunity" to share in the American dream. After his election he continued to argue that the problem of crime could not be divorced from the problems of poverty and education.

The politics of fear were beginning to take their toll on Johnson and the conservative Democrats in Congress. By 1965 Johnson had

TABLE 1.1 Respondents' Perception of the "Most Important Problem" Facing the United States, 1935–1997

Year	*Problem*
1935	Unemployment
1936	Unemployment
1937	Unemployment
1938	Keeping out of war
1939	Keeping out of war
1940	Keeping out of war
1941	Keeping out of war, winning war
1942	Winning war
1943	Winning war
1944	Winning war
1945	Winning war
1946	High cost of living
1947	High cost of living, labor unrest
1948	Keeping peace
1949	Labor unrest
1950	Labor unrest
1951	Korean War
1952	Korean War
1953	Keeping peace
1954	Keeping peace
1955	Keeping peace
1956	Keeping peace
1957	Race relations, keeping peace
1958	Unemployment, keeping peace
1959	Keeping peace
1960	Keeping peace
1961	Keeping peace
1962	Keeping peace
1963	Keeping peace, race relations
1964	Vietnam, race relations
1965	Vietnam, race relations
1966	Vietnam
1967	Vietnam, high cost of living
1968	Vietnam
1969	Vietnam
1970	Vietnam
1971	Vietnam, high cost of living
1972	Vietnam
1973	High cost of living, Watergate
1974	High cost of living, Watergate, energy crisis
1975	High cost of living, unemployment
1976	High cost of living, unemployment
1977	High cost of living, unemployment
1978	High cost of living, energy problem
1979	High cost of living, energy problem
1980	High cost of living, unemployment
1981	High cost of living, unemployment
1982	Unemployment, high cost of living
1983	Unemployment, high cost of living
1984	Unemployment, fear of war
1985	Fear of war, unemployment
1986	Unemployment, fear of war
1987	Fear of war, unemployment
1988	Budget deficit, drug abuse
1989	Drugs, poverty, homelessness
1990	Budget deficit, drugs
1991	Economy, poverty, homelessness, drugs, unemployment
1992	Economy, unemployment
1993	Health care, economy
1994	Crime/violence, health care
1995	Crime/violence, unemployment/jobs
1996[a]	Crime, drugs
1997	Crime/violence, drugs/drug abuse

SOURCES: Gallup Polls, 1935–1997

[a] 1996 data come from the *Los Angeles Times;* all other data come from Gallup.

conceded that "crime has become malignant energy in America's midst." He insisted, however, on putting the crime problem into a broader political-economic framework:

> We are not prepared in our democratic system to pay for improved law enforcement by unreasonable limitations on the individual protection which ennobles our system. Yet there is the undoubted necessity that society be protected from the criminal and that the rights of society be recognized along with the rights of the individual . . . the fault lies in poor living conditions, limited education, and the denial of opportunity. Plainly, laws are less likely to command the respect of those forced to live at the margins of our society. Stability and order have little meaning and small advantage to those who exist in poverty, hopelessness and despair.[6]

Johnson proposed legislation to establish the Office of Law Enforcement Assistance (OLEA) and the President's Commission on Law Enforcement and the Administration of Justice. He asked Congress for a $10 million grant for training law enforcement personnel and for the collection, evaluation, and dissemination of criminal justice information. In September 1965, Congress passed the bill and appropriated $7 million for each of the next three years.

The Republicans in Congress and aspiring Republican presidential candidates for the 1968 election continued to barrage the public with "law and order" campaigns built on racist stereotypes of violent, criminal black men out of control and out of reach of the law. As the 1966 congressional elections approached, the Republican party followed the Goldwater strategy of linking crime with civil rights. At a press conference on October 3, 1966, the Republican Coordinating Committee stated that "Unfortunately the Johnson-Humphrey Administration has accomplished nothing of substance to date to promote public safety. Indeed, high officials of this administration have condoned and encouraged disregard for law and order."[7] Richard Nixon jumped into the law and order fray with remarks previewing his upcoming presidential campaign: "A vote for Johnson's Congress is a vote for continuing the President's policy of no action against a crime rate which in the last half decade has grown six times as rapidly as the population."[8]

Despite the fact that the public was more concerned about war, civil rights, poverty, and unemployment, Republicans, conservative Democrats, and law enforcement spokespersons at every level of government continued to lobby for dramatic changes in the law and massive public expenditures to combat crime. There was vitriolic criticism of Supreme Court decisions, especially those protecting the rights of the accused. The *Miranda* decision, which required that statements made by suspects be voluntary if they were to be admissible in court, and *Gideon,* which gave every defendant a right to counsel, were fiercely criticized by conservative politicians and law enforcement officials.

The President's Crime Commission

President Johnson responded to the political pressure by appointing a blue-ribbon crime commission, which issued its report in February 1967. On the basis of the report, Johnson quickly proposed legislation that for the first time provided federal funds for local police. The centerpiece of the legislation was called the Safe Streets and Crime Control Act. Under this landmark legislation state and local governments continued to be the principal agents of law enforcement while the federal government provided funds to cities for planning, technical assistance, and research to aid in the fight against crime. By using the categorical grant approach (that is, allocating different amounts of matching funds for different programs), Johnson hoped to reduce the federal bureaucracy's power to dictate local law enforcement priorities and policies. This policy was to be turned on its head by subsequent administrations.

A Shift in the Focus of Concern

Both the House and Senate began hearings on the Safe Streets and Crime Control Act in the spring of 1967. By the time the bill was passed in 1968 its name had been changed to the Omnibus Crime Control and Safe Streets Act, and a coalition of conservative members of congress (five Democrats and three Republicans) had introduced several fundamental changes. First, the bill as passed provided grants to *states* rather than *cities.* Second, funds were now earmarked not for research on crime or for grants to train police officers but, rather, to create riot-control units. Third, the revised bill fundamentally altered previously guaranteed civil liberties by allowing federal agents and local police to carry out wiretapping and "bugging" without a court order. Fourth, the bill authorized judges to admit confessions as voluntary after considering "all factors," not just whether or not the confession was coerced. The *Miranda* decision required that suspects be told that they had right to remain silent and that anything they said could be held against them. By allowing judges to take into account "all factors" in deciding whether to allow defendants' statements as evidence, the bill gave judges the power to ignore the requirements of *Miranda.* Finally, the transformed bill exempted law enforcement agencies from having to meet the requirements of Title 6 of the 1964 Civil Rights Act, which denies federal grants to agencies or organizations that discriminate.

The spring of 1968 was a critical period in the development of the crime control industry. On March 31, 1968, President Johnson announced that he would not seek reelection. Four days later, Martin Luther King Jr. was murdered in Memphis, Tennessee, precipitating riots in more than a hundred cities across the United States. Millions of dollars' worth of property was destroyed and thirty-four people died. Two months later, Senator Robert Kennedy was assassinated while campaigning for the Democratic nomination.

In signing the Omnibus Crime Control and Safe Streets Act into law on June 19, 1968, President Johnson made significant concessions in his "War on Crime":

> In the end, the Administration's proposals suffered in three major ways: allocation of leadership responsibilities to the states rather than to the cities, congressional emphasis on tough crime control as opposed to reforms advocated by the Crime Commission and Ramsey Clark [the attorney general], and the decreased power of the Attorney General to control the operations of the new agency that was to administer the federal monies.[9]

In August 1968 a public opinion poll showed that 52 percent of those surveyed said the Vietnam War was the most important problem facing the United States, 29 percent named crime and lawlessness (including looting and riots), and 20 percent still called race relations the most pressing issue facing the nation.[10] This was the first time in more than thirty years that even a minority of those polled had mentioned crime as the most important national problem (see Table 1.1), and it followed on the heels of the riots and the assassinations of King and Kennedy. The next year, 1969, only 8 percent of respondents mentioned crime as the nation's most important problem. Fear of crime was clearly tied very closely to current events.

In the 1968 presidential campaign between Richard Nixon and Hubert H. Humphrey, Nixon and his running mate, Spiro Agnew, hammered away at the issue of law and order. It is ironic that two of the highest-ranking politicians in U.S. history exposed for systematic criminality while in office ran for election on a platform of "law and order." Vice President Spiro Agnew was convicted of accepting bribes and payoffs, and President Richard Nixon was forced to resign to avoid impeachment and consequent trial by the Senate for a host of crimes, including conspiracy to commit burglary and obstructing justice.

In a poorly veiled attempt to fan racist fears of the Civil Rights movement and the urban riots, Nixon followed Goldwater's lead and pursued

> [a] "southern strategy" for wresting electoral control of the Southern states from the Democratic party. At the heart of this strategy was an appeal to voters' fears of social unrest and violent crime. A major chord of the appeal was to sound especially on white fear of black street crime . . . It has been a staple ingredient of subsequent Republican electoral victories.[11]

Nixon attacked the Johnson administration's focus on social conditions as the cause of crime:

> By way of excuse, the present Administration places the blame on poverty. But poverty is just one contributing factor. During the Depression the crime rate was at an all-time low. The truth is that we will reduce crime and violence when we enforce our laws—when we make it less profitable, and a lot more risky to break them.[12]

Nixon held the Supreme Court partially responsible for the crime problem. He assailed some of the Court's decisions as having "tipped the balance against the peace forces and strengthened the criminal forces."[13] He stated, "The Supreme Court is not infallible.

It is sometimes wrong. Many of the decisions break down 5 to 4, and I think that often in recent years the five-man majority has been wrong and the four-man minority right. We need more strict constructionists on the highest court of the United States."[14] The Democratic candidate, Hubert Humphrey, expressed views on crime that were essentially the same as those Johnson had voiced in his campaign four years earlier: "Crime rates were highest among the poor and disadvantaged—who commit more crime but who also suffer more crime. In the long run we can only cut crime by getting at its cause: slums, unemployment, rundown schools and houses. This is where crime begins and that is where it must end."[15] Humphrey commented that Nixon's criticisms of Supreme Court decisions "lend themselves to a breakdown of law and order."[16]

In November 1968, Richard Nixon was elected president. The stage was set for the next major assault by conservative politicians and law enforcement agencies on "the crime problem."

Nixon, Congress, and the War on Crime

Nixon focused on organized crime to keep crime at the forefront of the political agenda and thus to provide a smoke screen for an assault on civil liberties. In his April 23, 1969, message to Congress, Nixon warned of the dangers of organized crime:

> It is vitally important that Americans see this alien organization for what it really is—a totalitarian and closed society operating within an open and democratic one. It has succeeded so far because an apathetic public is not aware of the threat it poses to American life. This public apathy has permitted most organized criminals to escape prosecution by corrupting officials, by intimidating witnesses and by terrorizing victims into silence.[17]

Nixon outlined several strategies in the fight against organized crime. He encouraged the attorney general to authorize widespread wiretapping of suspected organized crime figures. He also instructed the attorney general to establish twenty federal racketeering field offices. This institutionalized the experimental strike force teams that Henry Peterson, the chief of the Justice Department's Organized Crime and Racketeering Section, had established in 1966. Nixon asked Congress to approve a $300 million appropriation in the 1970 budget for the Law Enforcement Assistance Administration. Finally, Nixon encouraged Congress to pass the new legislation to be presented by the attorney general, most of which became part of the 1970 Organized Crime Control Act:

> From his studies in recent weeks, the Attorney General has concluded that new weapons and tools are needed to enable the Federal government to strike both the Cosa Nostra hierarchy and the sources of revenue that feed the coffers of organized crime. Accordingly, the Attorney General will ask Congress for new laws, and I urge Congress to act swiftly and favorably on the Attorney General's request.[18]

On January 15, 1969, conservative Democratic senators joined Republican conservatives to forge anticrime legislation. Senator John McClellan, along with the ranking members of the Senate Judiciary Subcommittee on Criminal Law and Procedures, introduced the Organized Crime Control Act (OCCA) in the Senate. Senator McClellan detailed his conception of the history and activities of organized crime and took the opportunity to comment on his vision of future law enforcement under Nixon. His speech made it clear that organized crime was only a smoke-screen behind which far-reaching legislation was being proposed: "It is my hope, that society will be . . . [given more protection] from . . . the assassin, the robber, the murderer, and the rapist than the Court has accorded to society in the past by some of its recent decisions."[19]

During hearings on the proposed legislation the American Civil Liberties Union (ACLU) criticized its impact on civil liberties:

> We find ourselves in the position of being critical of almost all of the proposals, and of each section of [the OCCA] . . . , because we think that not enough consideration has been given to constitutional rights in the desire to get at organized crime. It is all too easy when serious threats to our society arise to suggest the bending, the repealing perhaps, or the changing of traditional constitutional guarantees. We feel that this is a self-defeating kind of method and that the constitutional guarantees which have stood us in good stead during our past history should not be lightly set aside.[20]

Critics of the OCCA were not only concerned about constitutional issues but also distressed by the breadth of the legislation.

The OCCA, ostensibly intended as a weapon against organized crime, was in fact a broad, sweeping law that significantly increased police powers. Vincent Broderick of the New York Lawyers' Association pointed out that "While it is developed in the context of organized crime most of its provisions are going to have a broad, general application to everybody, to the organized criminal and to every other citizen who comes into contact one way or another with the law."[21]

Ignoring these warnings (or perhaps because of them), the Senate Judiciary Subcommittee on Criminal Laws and Procedures approved the OCCA two days later, by a roll-call vote of 73 to 1. Proposed amendments by Edward Kennedy (D.–Mass.) to restrict parts of the OCCA to organized crime and by Philip A. Hart (D.–Mich.) to eliminate a title of questionable constitutionality were defeated. The lone opposing vote was cast by Lee Metcalf (D.–Mont.). Metcalf, who was at that time regarded as one of the Senate's leading constitutional lawyers, told a reporter that he was aware of the political risks of voting against the OCCA but felt it was "the wrong way to curb crime to take away the basic rights of individuals."[22]

In the House, Representatives John Conyers Jr. (D.–Mich.), Abner J. Mikva (D.–Ill.), and William F. Ryan (D.–N.Y.) dissented when the bill was passed in the House by a vote of 341 to 26: "This bill is another dreary episode in the ponderous assault on freedom. It employs the spirit of repression extant in some quarters as a substitute for the Constitution, custom, and reason. And if all that were not enough, it won't work; it is more likely to catch poachers and prostitutes than it is to catch pushers and pimps."[23]

On October 15, 1970, President Nixon signed the OCCA into law at the Justice Department. Its ten titles contained some revolutionary changes in the administration of criminal law. Title 1 increased the powers of grand juries, Title 2 made it possible to compel witnesses to testify if they were granted limited immunity, and Title 3 allowed the district courts to incarcerate uncooperative witnesses for as long as the grand jury was in session. Title 9 (the RICO statute) prohibited involvement by racketeers in legitimate businesses. The OCCA allowed prosecutors to seize both the property of people caught with drugs and their parents' property. The bill's definition of "conspiracy" and of what constitutes a "criminal enterprise" were so general that the terms became almost meaningless: ". . . the definition of criminal 'enterprise' was so broad it could consist of one person. To be guilty of 'conspiracy,' a person didn't need actually to commit a crime; merely knowing about it, or being an active participant in the organization that committed it, was enough." A PBS documentary on informants described an Alabama case in which a twenty-two-year-old college student drove friends from one town to another, where the friends purchased drugs. The college student was found guilty of conspiracy and sentenced to life in prison, even though he neither purchased nor used any of the drugs. The RICO statute was the legal grounds for the prosecution.

Title 10, which increased the sentences of recidivist offenders, may have been the most important section of the OCCA. It was a precursor of things to come. Twenty years later the logic of longer sentences for recidivists would result in mandatory minimum sentences and "three strikes and you're out" laws.

Nixon's War on Crime was extended during his term in office to include a War on Drugs. During his administration, for the first time, a federal role was established in local law enforcement.

Recent Legislation

The legislation of the late 1960s and early 1970s began a trend toward "getting tough on crime" that has continued unabated through both Republican and Democratic administrations. Any chance that Democratic party candidates would adopt the Johnson-Humphrey theme of fighting poverty and increasing opportunities as a way to combat crime was dashed in the 1988 presidential campaign between Michael Dukakis and George Bush. In the midst of that campaign Willie Horton, a black man who was on furlough from a Massachusetts prison, raped a white woman. Bush was quick to blame Dukakis, a former governor of Massachusetts, for allowing dangerous criminals to be released from prison. Political analysts agree that this incident contributed to George Bush's victory.

Four years later, when Arkansas governor Bill Clinton ran against George Bush, he quickly established the War on Crime as a major tenet of his campaign. To demonstrate his commitment to getting tough on crime, Clinton interrupted his campaign travel to return to Arkansas to witness the execution of a mentally retarded inmate.

A steady stream of laws has (1) added hundreds of new federal crimes, (2) steadily increased expenditures on crime control, (3) increased the severity of penalties for virtually all kinds of crimes, (4) revolutionized the role of judges and juries by providing mandatory minimum sentences for first-time as well as repeat offenders, and (5) moved steadily toward trying and incarcerating juveniles as adults. As always, it is politics that drives the frenzy. (See Box 1.1.)

In 1986 Len Bias signed a contract with the Boston Celtics basketball team. Before he could play a game with his new team, however, he died of an overdose of drugs. When Tip O'Neill (D.–Mass.), a powerful member of Congress, went back to his district for the Fourth of July recess, Len Bias's death was front-page news. According to Eric Sterling, who was counsel to the House Subcommittee on Crime chaired by Tip O'Neill,

> Tip O'Neill came back from the July 4th District Recess and everybody's talking about the Boston Celtic's player Len Bias who died of a drug overdose. And he [O'Neill] has this insight: Drugs. It's drugs. I can take this issue into the election. And he calls the Democratic leadership together in the House of Representatives and tells them he wants a drug bill in four weeks. Everybody is trying to get out front on the drug issue and it sets off a kind of stampede. Every committee, Merchant Marines, Fisheries, Foreign Affairs, Agriculture, Armed Services, Ways and Means—not just the Judiciary Committee. Everybody's fighting to get their face on television and is talking about the drug problem.[24]

In the rush to make political hay in the last two days before the summer 1986 recess, Congress passed laws setting mandatory minimum sentences for drug offenders. Sterling continued: "There were no hearings, no consideration of the views of federal judges. No input from the Bureau of Prisons. Even the Drug Enforcement Administration didn't testify. The whole thing was kind of cobbled together with chewing gum and baling wire." Since 1986 the War on Drugs has led to an astronomical increase in the number of people in prison and has consumed hundreds of billions of dollars of

BOX 1.1 Senseless Sentencing: A Federal Judge Speaks Out

Robert W. Pratt, U.S. District Court Judge for the Southern District of Iowa
Des Moines Register, January 10, 1999

On December 17, 1998, nine of my fellow citizens appeared before me in Davenport (Iowa), for sentencing on drug charges. The cost to U.S. taxpayers for incarcerating one person for one month in federal prisons is $1,910.17. Based on the nine sentences I had to impose under the largely mandatory Federal Sentencing Guidelines, taxpayers were handed a bill of more than $2 million.

There are approximately 650 federal judges across the United States responsible for sentencing drug offenders. If sentencing nine offenders in Davenport, IA, on one day cost more than $2 million, the effect of 649 other judges doing the same thing across the nation on a daily basis is mind-boggling.

Federal judges used to have wide discretion to fashion sentences they thought were appropriate for the individual and the circumstances of the offense—to "make the punishment fit the crime." However, there is evidence that allowing federal judges and parole boards absolute discretion allowed personal temperament and prejudices to play a part in sentencing. As University of Chicago law professor Albert Alschuler has pointed out, there are both Santa Clauses and Scrooges on the bench, but more troubling were statistics showing that the length of time actually served often pointed to discrimination based on race, class, or gender—and punishment should not turn on the luck of the judicial draw. In response to this legitimate problem Congress established the U.S. Sentencing Commission to create official guidelines that would result in more uniform punishments. The sentencing guidelines abolish parole and set a mandatory, narrow range, in months, for sentences based only on the particular crime committed and the criminal history of the defendant.

In addition, Congress created "mandatory-minimum sentences" for some crimes, which trump or replace the guideline sentences and require the imposition of specified prison terms for the commission of certain enumerated crimes, including drug crimes.

Costly, Ineffective

There is very little judicial discretion in the current system. While the concern of disparity in sentencing is legitimate, the move from individualized sentences to mandatory ones has proved costly and ineffective.

I have only been a Federal judge for a short time. In that time, however, I have learned that sentencing offenders under the guidelines is an emotionally draining experience that requires consideration of the crime and past conduct of the defendant. Consideration must also be given to the effect of guideline sentencing on our country. What have we done by creating a system that many federal judges have rejected as unfair, inefficient, and, as a practical matter, ineffective in eliminating drug use and drug-related crime?

taxpayer money in a vain attempt to control the American people's use of some (but not all) mind-altering substances.

Mandatory sentences are now specified for more than a hundred federal and state crimes. Thirty-one states followed the federal lead in enacting "three strikes and you're out" laws, which require judges to sentence offenders to life in prison on a third felony conviction for a felony, no matter how petty the crime. More than a hundred federal offenses are now subject to the death penalty.

In their zealousness to take the crime issue away from the Republicans, Democrats under Clinton have proved they can be more reactionary than their opponents. Clinton made crime a centerpiece of both the 1988 and the 1992 campaigns, and on this issue, unlike the issue of medical care for all Americans, he delivered. In 1994 he signed into law a bill allocating almost $24 billion to enable local law enforcement agencies to add 100,000 new police officers and $7.9 billion to construct new state prisons. In 1998 Clinton announced that the Justice Department would provide additional money for eighteen U.S. cities that had not experienced a decline in the crime rate to hire seven hundred more police officers. Such funding amounted to rewarding failure and encouraged cities to present slanted statistics. And in Clinton's 1999 State of the Union message, crime took center stage again as he promised to provide funds for an additional 60,000 police officers. There are, of course, strings attached to these funds: State and municipal governments must agree to follow federal sentencing guidelines, including mandatory minimum sentences. During Clinton's presidency the allocation of funds for the War on Drugs tripled, and the severity of sentences for even possession of minor amounts of drugs soared.

The Consequences

Crime has been raised to the level of a national crisis by a coalition of interests (sometimes strange bedfellows, to be sure) including (1) conservative politicians concerned primarily with repressing civil rights activism and political dissent; (2) the media, ever hungry to attract readers and viewers with issues that captivate the imagination and fears of the public; and (3) the law enforcement establishment, with an insatiable appetite for public funds and public approval.

Despite having been waged for almost thirty years, the campaign begun in 1964 to convince Americans that they are under siege from criminals has not completely succeeded. The Gallup polls of the 1980s continued to show that only a small portion of respondents viewed crime as "the most important problem facing the country." In fact, it was not until 1994 that Americans began consistently telling pollsters that they thought crime was a significant problem. This is not surprising given that, as pointed out in the Introduction, very few Americans are the victims of crime and the vast majority feel that the neighborhood *where they themselves live* is safe. The brainwashing of America did not make people fearful of their own neighborhoods; it only made them believe that "out there" in the ghetto there were neighborhoods where crime was rampant.

The campaign did succeed, however, in much more important ways. The anticrime campaign begun by conservative Republicans and Democrats legitimized the passage of Draconian laws and the rapid expansion of the crime control industry. Between 1980 and 1999 expenditures on criminal justice and the number of police officers in the United States more than doubled. (See Table 1.2.)

The allocation of public funds for policing has not only siphoned scarce resources away from education, welfare, and other social expenditures, the wars on crime and drugs have also led to the institutionalization of racism by defining the crime problem as a problem of young black men and women. Racial repression through law, in turn, is being met with increased estrangement, hostility, loss of hope, and acts of violence against white society. When police officers accused of assaulting Rodney King were tried in a white suburban court by a jury of ten whites, one Hispanic, one Filipino, but no blacks, riots broke out in Atlanta; Seattle; Madison, Wisconsin; and Los Angeles. As a result, LA experienced the most costly and deadliest riot in U.S. history, resulting in more than $1 billion in property damage, 54 people killed, and more than 2,000 people injured.

The issue of crime was raised for political purposes and was perpetuated by groups with a vested interest in elevating crime to the level of a national crisis. The political process culminated in some of the most far-reaching pieces of criminal legislation in recent history,

TABLE 1.2 Expenditures on Criminal Justice and Law Enforcement Officers, 1980–2000

Federal grants for state and local law enforcement	
1995: $45 million	1999: $1.241 billion
State and local expenditures on criminal justice	
1985: $49 million	1993: $98 million
State and local law enforcement employees	
1975: 344,089	1996: 829,838
State and local law enforcement employees per 1,000 residents	
1975: 2.5	1996: 3.0
Federal budget for the War on Drugs	
1980: $1 billion	1999: $17 billion
Operating costs of state and federal prisons	
1992: $15.1 billion	2000 (estimated) $133 billion

including the Omnibus Crime Control and Safe Streets Act, the Organized Crime Control Act, mandatory minimum sentencing, and "three strikes and you're out" laws. Contrary to the conventional wisdom of social science, these laws were not passed as a consequence of any widespread societal panic about crime. Indeed, it is closer to the mark to say that since 1964 "the crime problem" has been forced on a reluctant public and did not reflect their views.

During the 1960s the U.S. Congress was dominated by conservative forces refusing to confront the issues that were uppermost in the minds of the public: the Vietnam War, poverty, civil rights, unemployment, and race relations. Instead, in response to the civil rights and antiwar demonstrations and the "liberal" decisions of the Warren Supreme Court, Congress implemented laws that would increase the repressiveness of the criminal justice system.

Between 1964 and 1999 conservative legislators, law enforcement agencies, and the media together created a panic about crime in the United States. One consequence was the passage of criminal laws that strengthened the federal law enforcement effort in relation to the states. Another was an increase in police powers to deal with political dissidents, civil rights activists, and other protesters (ironically, including antiabortion protesters). Most important, however, the panic and the laws have legitimized a level of oppression of young black men in the ghetto that is devastating to the community and especially to a generation of black and Hispanic males, who have become stigmatized as members of a "dangerous class."

Draconian legislation has continued unchecked as the severity of sentences creates a self-perpetuating criminal justice–industrial complex that is rapidly rivaling the military-industrial complex as a bottomless pit into which tax dollars are poured.

The politicians were supported by a staunch ally in creating panic over crime: the law enforcement bureaucracies. Throughout the period from 1960 to the mid-1990s the law enforcement establishment provided the media and the politicians with grist for their mill,[25] publishing lies and distortions about the extent and seriousness of crime, a subject to which I turn in Chapter 2.

Notes

This chapter was coauthored with Edward Sbarbaro, of the Graduate School of Public Policy, University of Colorado, Colorado Springs.

1. Quoted in Thomas E. Cronin, Tania I. Cronin, Michael E. Milakomich, *United States Crime in the Streets* (Bloomington: Indiana University Press, 1981), 18.

2. "Text of Goldwater's Speech Formally Opening Presidential Campaign," *New York Times*, September 4, 1964, 12.

3. "Johnson Calls Medicare Law His Top 1965 Goal," *New York Times*, October 25, 1964, 81.

4. "The Curious Campaign—Point by Point," *Newsweek*, October 19, 1964, 27–34.

5. *Congressional Quarterly Guide*, Spring 1965, 5–8.

6. Lyndon Johnson, *Public Papers of the President of the United States: Containing the Public Messages, Speeches, and Statements of the President 1963/1964–1968/1969: Lyndon Johnson 1963–1969* (Washington, D.C.: GPO, 1965–1970), vol. 2, book 1, 1965, 265.

7. "G.O.P. Will Press Racial Disorders as Election Issue," *New York Times*, October 4, 1966, 1.

8. "Nixon Urges Parties to Confer with Johnson on War Strategy," *New York Times*, November 1, 1966, 1.

9. Cronin, Cronin, and Milakomich, *United States Crime in the Streets*, 49.

10. George Gallup, *The Gallup Poll: Public Opinion, 1935–1997* (New York: Random House, 1998), 2107.

11. Chris Bryson, "Crime Pays for Those in the Prison Business," *The National Times*, September 1996, 31.

12. "Urban Issues Dominate Candidates' Domestic Views," *New York Times,* October 25, 1968, 34.
13. "Nixon Urges Four Steps to Curb Nation's Crime," *New York Times,* September 30, 1968, 1.
14. "Nixon Intensifies Blows at Humphrey on Train Tour," *New York Times,* October 23, 1968, 1.
15. "Excerpts from Humphrey Text Dealing with Crime," *New York Times,* September 12, 1968, 1.
16. "Humphrey Terms Nixon a Wiggler on Criminal Issues," *New York Times,* September 12, 1968, 1.
17. Measures Relating to Organized Crime Hearings Before the Subcommittee on Criminal Laws and Procedures of the Committee on the Judiciary: U.S. Senate, 91st Cong., 1st sess., March 18, 19, 25 and June 3, 4, 1969, 444.
18. Ibid., 448.
19. Ibid., 512.
20. Ibid., 479.
21. Ibid., 239.
22. *Congressional Quarterly Almanac, 1969* (Washington, D.C.: GPO, 1970), 77, 549; "Senate Approves Measure To Fight Organized Crime," *New York Times,* January 24, 1970, 14.
23. House of Representatives *Organized Crime Control Act of 1970,* report no. 91-1549, September 30, 1970. Report together with individual and dissenting views, 181.
24. "The Snitch," PBS *Frontline,* Tuesday, January 12, 1999.
25. Melissa Hickman Barton, David E. Barlow, and Theadore G. Chirisos, "Economic Conditions and Ideologies of Crime in the Media," *Crime and Delinquency* 41, no. 1 (1995): 3–19.

Chapter Two

Marketing Crime: The Politics of Crime Statistics

In his farewell address as president Dwight Eisenhower warned, "We must guard against the acquisition of unwarranted influence, whether sought or unsought, by the military-industrial complex. The potential for the disastrous rise of misplaced power exists and will persist." An equally honest and observant politician in the United States today would warn of the emergence of an all-powerful law enforcement–industrial complex for many of the same reasons Eisenhower noted. First, like the military after World War II, the law enforcement–industrial complex is growing faster than any other government function, including education. Government is downsizing and budgets are being slashed, but law enforcement agencies are enjoying unprecedented growth.

In only a four-year period, federal grants for state and local law enforcement increased by an incredible 2,758 percent, growing from $45 million in 1995 to $1.241 billion in 1999.[1] Between 1979 and 1996 annual expenditures on criminal justice grew by more than $70 billion.[2] States now spend more than $20 billion a year on corrections (that is, prisons) alone. Between 1980 and 1999 the average state operating budgets going to corrections increased from 2 percent to 6 percent.[3] The federal budget for the War on Drugs increased from $1 billion in 1980 to more than $17 billion for 1999;

at the current rate of expenditures the criminal justice budget will exceed $200 billion by 2005.

Prisons for Profit

The law enforcement–industrial complex is sustaining some of the fastest-growing corporations and some of the most-powerful lobbies in the country. Providing equipment to law enforcement agencies and food for 2 million prisoners is a huge industry. In addition, states are increasingly turning over the ownership and management of prisons to private corporations. Whereas in 1985 there were fewer than 1,000 inmates housed in privately run prisons, by 1999 there were more than 70,000 inmates incarcerated in more than 100 private prisons in nineteen states. One of the largest corporations running private prisons is the Corrections Corporation of America (CCA). It currently operates or has under construction facilities with more than 30,000 beds in forty-seven prisons throughout the United States, Puerto Rico, Britain, and Australia. So profitable is the CCA that in 1995 its common stock rose 385 percent, and a major investment newsletter published an article, "Crime Can Pay," recommending these stocks.[4]

Pursuing the same incestuous policies employed by defense contractors, who hire former defense department officials and retired military personnel, private prison corporations hire ex–government officials who are allegedly experts in security. Michael Quinlon, former director of the Federal Bureau of Prisons is a director at CCA, a former commissioner of corrections for Arkansas founded CCA, and a former chairman of the Tennessee Republican Party (Tom Beasley) is on the board of directors. The Wackenhut Corporation—which provided security for the National Aeronautics and Space Administration (NASA), the Department of Energy, and other government agencies—has formed a subsidiary called the Wackenhut Corrections Corporation. Its board of directors has included William Casey, former director of the CIA; Bobby Ray Inman, former deputy director of the CIA; and William Raborn, former head of the CIA. In addition, right-wing political leaders, such as George Mas Canos of the ultra-right-wing Cuban American Foundation, serve on the board.[5]

CCA and Wackenhut make substantial political contributions, which promises to keep the movement toward the privatization of prisons alive and well for a long time to come. Prison guards also represent a formidable lobby: The California Corrections Officers Association was the largest contributor to conservative Pete Wilson's winning gubernatorial campaign. On a local level, police unions, under various innocuous names like the Police Benevolent Society and the Fraternal Order of Police, are major contributors to the campaigns of politicians who promise more funding for law enforcement. They also provide backdrops for photo ops for sympathetic politicians and run ads attacking politicians who dare interfere with police budget and manpower increases.

Crime Statistics

Much like in the 1950s, when silence surrounded the military-industrial complex, there is little opposition among politicians, in the media, or by the public to criminal justice spending. In fact, as we shall see, the only source of information about the crime problem and how to solve it comes from the agencies and corporations that stand to benefit from exaggerating and distorting the information.

In 1931 a federal commission, known as the Wickersham Commission, was appointed to study the need for a national system of crime reporting. Its final report warned of the dangers inherent in having the law enforcement agencies with a vested interest in the policies based on crime data responsible for gathering that data. Referring to the fact that the data for the *Uniform Crime Reports* are gathered and disseminated by the FBI, the commission concluded:

> Nothing can be more misleading than statistics not scientifically gathered and compiled. The Uniform Crime Reports . . . [the FBI's annual summary of crime in the United States] make no suggestion as to any limitations or doubts with respect to the utility or authority of the figures presented. On the contrary they contain a graphic chart of "monthly crime trends," and along with them the bureau has released to the press statements quoting and interpreting them without qualification. It requires no great study of these reports to perceive a number of weaknesses which should impose a more cautious promulgation of them.[6]

Unfortunately, the warnings of the Wickersham Commission were ignored, and the Department of Justice and the FBI are the only source of data on crime. They, however, are not disinterested observers of crime trends; rather, they are bureaucracies with a vested interest in misleading the public.

The *Uniform Crime Reports*

In an effort to take a bite out of the budgets of other governmental agencies, the Department of Justice and its law enforcement bureaucracies, especially the FBI and the National Institutes of Justice, consistently inflate or bias reports of data on crime. These same federal agencies hand out lucrative research grants to criminologists who uncritically accept the Department of Justice's crime control perspective.

But of all the misleading and distorted information about crime, none is more damaging than the oldest established source of national data on crime rates and trends: the FBI's annual *Uniform Crime Reports* (*UCR*). These reports are based on data supplied to the FBI by local police departments. They include information on crime trends, the seriousness of crimes committed, and expenditures on criminal justice; arrest data; and data on the number of people employed in police work. Crime rates and crime trends are based on "crimes known to the police," which reflect calls to police departments from citizens reporting crimes and crimes observed by police officers.[7]

The FBI is masterful in disseminating its information. News releases are carefully prepared to highlight the most alarming statistics that can be culled from the reports. These releases are sent to every newspaper in every city and town of the fifty states. The reports themselves are widely distributed, and they are constructed to give the media ready access to crime clocks, graphs, and tables designed to spread the FBI's propaganda. The media, for its part, uncritically accepts as incontestable fact the data provided by the FBI. In reality, the *UCR* is neither incontestable nor fact.

In its reports and news releases, the FBI uses gimmicks and tricks to make the problem of crime seem as threatening as possible. For example, somewhere in the first few pages of the annual *UCR* there appears a "crime clock." This picture of a twenty-four-hour clock purports to show, in seconds and minutes, how often particular crimes occur. In the 1998 *UCR*, for example, the clock showed a murder occurring every twenty-seven minutes, a forcible rape every six minutes, a robbery every fifty-nine seconds, a burglary every thirteen seconds, and so on.[8] Rendering the data this way exaggerates the seriousness and frequency of crime. To get these alarming numbers the FBI includes all kinds of alleged and attempted crimes that, if more honestly conveyed, would not be counted. Furthermore, the number of crimes per second or minute obviously depends on the size of the population being surveyed. Imagine what a similar chart for China, India, or Indonesia would look like. Such representations are not informative; they are simply political rhetoric.

The *UCR* is consistent in only one thing: its tendency to distort and mislead. In 1992 the front cover of the *UCR* contained a rising graph (Figure 2.1). Under the graph appear the words "Crime in the United States." Clearly the cover is designed to depict a rapidly accelerating crime rate. The data provided to the FBI, however, tell a very different story. The crime rate for most major crimes actually went down. From 1991 to 1992, the overall crime rate declined by 4.0 per 100,000 population and the homicide rate declined by 5.1 per 100,000 population. To discover that the crime rate declined, however, the reader had to look past the cover, past the introductory statements, and past the crime clocks—something few politicians, journalists, or government bureaucrats bother to do.

Counting Crimes

The way crimes are counted is no less misleading than the graphs and clocks. For example, FBI instructions to local police departments direct that if a police officer finds a dead body and believes the person was murdered, the event is recorded as a murder. It matters not if the next day the coroner says it was a suicide or the prosecutor later determines it was a justifiable homicide or an accidental death. The incident remains a murder for the purposes of the *UCR*. The instructions state, ". . . the findings of coroner, court, jury or prosecutor do not unfound offenses or attempts which your [police] investigations establish to be legitimate."[9] That this way of counting grossly exaggerates the murder rate is suggested by the fact that whereas the FBI reports about 20,000 murders every

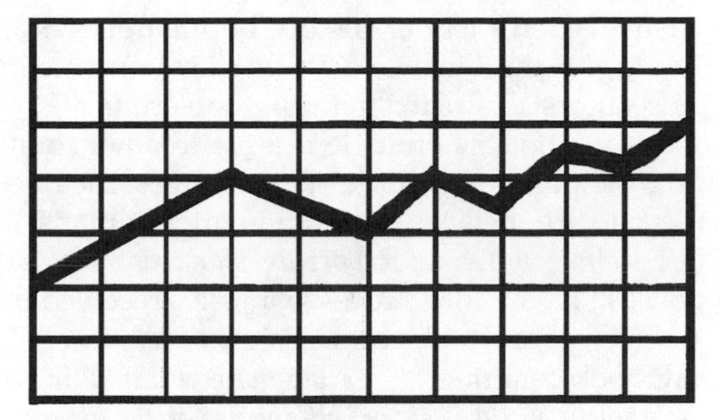

FIGURE 2.1 Crime in the United States, 1992

(No Dates, No Rates) This figure, which had no data, just a line across a graph, appeared on the front cover of the 1992 *Uniform Crime Reports* above the bold statement CRIME IN THE UNITED STATES; it suggests that the crime rate is going steadily upward. In fact, the data in the report showed that the crime rate declined by 4.0 per 100,000 population between 1991 and 1992, the dates covered by the report.

SOURCE: *Uniform Crime Reports.*

year,[10] there are fewer than 13,000 convictions in state and federal courts for murder and nonnegligent manslaughter combined.[11]

A surefire tactic to generate fear in Americans is to compare the U.S. homicide rate with that of other countries. Whenever law enforcement officials, politicians, or judges want to justify "getting tough on crime," they roll out the timeworn comparisons supposedly demonstrating that the murder rate in the United States is dramatically higher than in any other industrialized nation, especially the Scandinavian countries. In a speech at the National Press Club, for example, former Chief Justice of the Supreme Court Warren Burger fanned the flames of fear and called for tougher laws by pointing out that Sweden, with a population of 6 million, had fewer homicides than Washington, D.C., with a population of 650,000.

These comparisons are not only distorted, they are irresponsible. To continue the example, in Sweden a death is not officially recorded as a murder *until someone has been found guilty in court of having committed the crime.* By that standard, the U.S. murder rate for 1996 would be approximately 3.5 per 100,000 population—a rate higher than Sweden's 1.1 per 100,000 population, certainly, but hardly justifying the chief justice's alarmist statements or politicians' and prosecutors' desire to "get tough on crime."[12]

Most comparisons of U.S. homicide rates with other countries are like comparing the proverbial apples and oranges. Included in the U.S. homicide rate are instances of "nonnegligent manslaughter," which the FBI's *Uniform Crime Reporting Handbook* instructs local police to report as ". . . any death due to injuries received in a fight, argument, quarrel, assault, or commission of a crime." Furthermore, the handbook continues, ". . . *Do not count a killing as justifiable or excusable solely on the basis of self-defense or the action of a coroner, prosecutor, grand jury, or court.* The willful (nonnegligent) killing of one individual by another is being reported, not the criminal liability of the person or persons involved [emphasis in original]."[13]

The FBI's maximization of crime prevalence is not limited to homicide. The *Uniform Crime Reporting Handbook* instructs police departments to count each person who commits a crime as a separate incident and each victim as a separate incident. If five men are picked up for fighting with five others, the police report ten aggravated assaults. If three men are involved in one carjacking, three carjackings are counted. If one man attacks five others in a bar, the incident is counted as five aggravated assaults: "If a number of persons are involved in a dispute or disturbance and police investigation cannot establish the aggressors from the victims, count the number of persons assaulted as the number of offenses."[14] In other words, if it is unclear who, if anyone, involved in a fight has committed a crime, the official statistics will show the number of people assaulted as the number of crimes. The instructions do not require that the legal definition of assault be met in order for the incident to be reported as such. A simple "dispute or disturbance" may be counted. In this context, no charges need ever be brought. Though police officers may be unwilling to arrest someone for assault simply for being involved in a "dispute or disturbance," the failure to make an arrest does not keep the incident from being reported as a crime (in this case a violent crime) known to the police. If several people are assaulted by one person, in a bar fight for example, each assault is counted. For example, if four people in a bar get into a fight, the owner calls the police—who come to the bar and quell the fight—no one is arrested, and no one presses charges, the police still report four aggravated assaults to the FBI. The four assaults are included in the FBI's calculation of the violent crime rate.

The categories in the *UCR* are anything but "uniform." What counts as burglary in one jurisdiction may not in another. Burglary is legally defined in many states as the use of force for breaking and entering, but the FBI instructs local police departments in all states to report the crime of burglary simply if there is unlawful entry. Merging unlawful entry with breaking and entering makes statistics on "burglary" ambiguous and, of course, *increases* the number of burglary offenses reported.

What constitutes an attempted crime (rape, robbery, or assault, for example) also varies from jurisdiction to jurisdiction and from police officer to police officer. The fact that "attempts" are included in the overall rate for every type of crime but murder further confounds the data, making it impossible to interpret them in any meaningful way.

Dirty Tricks

J. Edgar Hoover was a master at manipulating public opinion. He held the media in the palm of his hand and fed them whatever served his interests. For years he even went so far as to claim that the FBI did not cost the taxpayer anything, since, he claimed, the amount it recovered annually in stolen property was more than its annual budget.

To be able to make this astonishing claim, Hoover relied on the FBI's enforcement of the Dyer Act. The Dyer Act (1919) made the interstate transportation of stolen cars a federal crime. The law was intended to help prosecute full-time commercial car thieves. The FBI, however, focused on "joyriders," young men who stole cars on a casual, spur-of-the-moment basis. (More than 90 percent of automobile thefts are joyrides: The car is stolen, driven around, usually for less than twenty-four hours, and abandoned.) These cases are "solved" not by remarkable police work but by locating the abandoned car. The FBI, however, counted the recovery of all stolen vehicles as part of the cases they "solved."

According to Harry Subin, a professor of law at New York University, ". . . the whole federal auto-theft program was part of a fraudulent effort by Hoover's FBI to polish its image. It's clear that

Dyer Act investigations are of primary importance in the Bureau's evaluation of its overall accomplishments."[15]

The huge number of automobile theft cases the FBI handled enabled Hoover not only to demonstrate the FBI's diligence in solving serious property crimes but also to claim that the FBI was *profitable.* By counting the estimated cost of stolen automobiles returned to their owners as money "returned to the government," the FBI could claim that it returned more money to the government than its appropriation. Unless all the vehicles returned by the FBI were government-owned, this claim is nothing but sleight-of-hand accounting. Any such scam perpetrated by the CEO of a bank would be considered outright fraud.

Hoover established a tradition that every FBI director since has followed. When the present FBI director, Louis J. Freeh, was appointed, he addressed the nation over C-Span, National Public Radio, and the Internet. In his address he pursued the same distorted, misleading, and alarmist approach to the crime problem that had so well served his many predecessors: "The rate of violent crimes has increased 371 percent since 1960—that's nine times faster than our population has grown. In the past 30 years, homicides have nearly tripled, robberies and rapes each are up over 500 percent, aggravated assaults have increased more than 600 percent."[16] Freeh came up with these alarming statistics by carefully choosing a year—1992—that had one of the lowest homicide rates in sixty years and comparing it with the year that had the highest reported homicide rate in the same sixty-year period. Even using the FBI data on homicide, which as we have seen are highly suspect, a more honest depiction of changing homicide rates would show that it ebbs and flows from year to year. One could just as easily compare data from 1992 to data from 1978 to demonstrate that the homicide rate had gone down in the fourteen-year period preceding Freeh's appointment as director. But this comparison would serve neither his interests nor the interests of the ever-hungry-for-expansion bureaucracy he heads.

When Crime Rates Decline

Budget processes at state and federal levels being what they are, law enforcement agencies generally try to show how bad crime is to justify increased allocations and bloated budgets.

Occasionally, however, the reverse happens: Political winds shift and a savvy mayor, governor, or head of a law enforcement bureaucracy decides to show how effective their policies are. To demonstrate this, the police are under pressure to show a decline in the crime rate. In recent years the crime rate has declined for several reasons. The bottom line, however, is that declines in the crime rate reported by law enforcement agencies are no more reliable than alleged increases.

Beginning in the 1990s most major cities in the United States began reporting dramatic declines in violent crime rates. New York was the first city to report substantial declines.

After his election as mayor of New York, Rudolph Giuliani, himself a former prosecuting attorney, directed his police commissioner to establish a way of informing precinct commanders precisely where crime was occurring in their jurisdictions. The police commissioner established a computerized database, and every four or five weeks each precinct commander was brought into central headquarters and shown a computer display of where and how many crimes occurred in his precinct in the past month. He was instructed to get the rates down. Not surprisingly, most of the commanders got the rates down. Those who didn't were reprimanded.

Following Giuliani's example, mayors and police chiefs throughout the country were under pressure to also reduce the crime rate, especially the violent crime rate. In what can only be considered a miracle, crime rates began declining in almost every big city. By the late 1990s the rates were being heralded as demonstrating the success of get-tough laws and a host of other crime fighting strategies, including more police officers.

There is evidence, however, that the crime rate's downward drift is explained at least in part by a combination of sleight-of-hand statistical manipulation on the part of local police and the natural tendency of crime rates to go up and down from one period of time to another.

In New York, while the reported homicide rate was declining, the reported rate of both accidental deaths and suicides was increasing. Which raises the possibility that part of the decline was due to police simply changing their designation of "cause of death" from homicide to suicide or accidental death.

Homicide statistics are based on local police department reports to the FBI. For the purposes of reporting the cause of death to the FBI homicide is defined thus: "Any death due to injuries received in a fight, argument, quarrel, assault, or commission of a crime *do not count a killing as justifiable or excusable solely on the basis of self-defense or the action of a coroner, prosecutor, grand jury, or court*."?[17]

A coroner, prosecutor, grand jury, or court can declare that a death was not a homicide, but if the police officer investigating the death says on the initial examination of the scene that it was a homicide, then it is a homicide that is reported to the FBI. This not only produces an extremely unreliable index of homicide; it also opens wide the possibility for manipulating the data as dictated by organizational interests. With Mayor Giuliani publicizing his get-tough-on-crime platform and simultaneously demanding that police reduce crime, it is not surprising that homicide rates declined. Accidental deaths, suicides, as well as justifiable or excusable killings can easily be shifted in and out of homicide reports to raise or lower the homicide rate at will. Given the political pressures to lower crime rates, it would be a surprise if the violent crime rate did not decline.

Once the crime rate, especially the violent crime rate, declined in New York other big-city mayors and police chiefs were under intense pressure to demonstrate that they, too, could get the crime rate in their cities lower as well. One by one across the nation, with each city following New York's example, crime rates began declining in Houston, Los Angeles, Washington, D.C., Chicago, and Baltimore. The *Uniform Crime Reports*, of course, reflected these changes and began reporting a decline in crime rates as well. It is, however, quite curious to say the least that this trend in declining crime rates spread annually from one city to the next only after New York's highly publicized success at lowering the crime rate.

The ensuing euphoria was dampened somewhat by numerous reports of police manipulating crime data to show lower crime rates. In New York, Philadelphia, and Atlanta reports surfaced of falsified numbers. This was accomplished mainly by lowering the seriousness of the crime reported: Aggravated assaults became simple assaults, burglaries became trespasses, and, as mentioned above, deaths normally reported as homicides were reported as due to accidents, suicides, cause of death unknown, or negligent manslaughter.

The city of Baltimore conducted one of the few systematic efforts to determine if lowered crime rates were artifacts of police manipulation. When a new mayor was elected in 1998 he appointed a commission to investigate whether the crime rate actually had gone down as was claimed during the administration of the previous mayor. The commission found that police had intentionally been downgrading offenses so that the crime rate would go down. A vehicle that had its car window smashed and was ransacked was categorized as destruction of property rather than attempted theft. In one case a woman was thrown to the ground and cut by a masked man wielding a piece of broken glass. The police reported this as a simple assault rather than an aggravated assault or attempted rape.

The commission reviewed hundreds of cases of this sort and concluded that the serious crime rate had actually gone up by 3.5 percent rather than declining by 14 percent as previously reported.

When the gathering and reporting of crime rate data is in the hands of the bureaucracies whose public image and financial well-being depend on what the statistics look like, it is safe to assume that the agencies' data are suspect. Until we have an independent agency gathering and reporting crime data, we are subject to the propaganda of local and federal law enforcement agencies.

Police and Prosecutors' Charges

In the United States more than 90 percent of the criminal cases brought to court are settled by a guilty plea obtained as the result of a bargaining process in which the prosecuting attorney confronts the accused with the charges and warns him or her of the possible dire consequences of being found guilty of these charges. In order to expedite the case, the prosecuting attorney offers to accept a guilty plea to a lesser charge, carrying a less severe punishment, than the charges brought by the police. The official statistics, however, report the *most serious crime* charged, not the crime for which the defendant eventually pleads or is found guilty.

The charges actually brought against the defendant may not reflect the reality of what transpired. Knowing that plea bargaining will take place, police officers and prosecutors exaggerate the charges in order to disadvantage the defendant in the bargaining process and to increase the likelihood that the defendant will plead guilty to a lesser charge. A case in point is that of Willie Butts (a pseudonym) who was arrested late at night walking down an alley in Jacksonville, Florida. Butts was charged with "possession of controlled substance (crack), resisting arrest with violence and battery of law enforcement officer." The arresting officer's report states:

> The investigation revealed that on 06-06-87 at about 0020 I saw a vehicle drive to the 800 block of [———] street from [———]. Its lights off, stopped and talked to someone. The person drove off in less than one minute. I then drove to that area without lights. When I saw someone walk up to my vehicle, I turned on my lights to confront the suspect. As I began to exit my vehicle, the suspect reached into his front left pocket, pulled out a crack pipe and cigarette pack and threw it behind him to the ground. As I attempted to place the suspect against my car, he threw another object across the top of my car. When I attempted to search the suspect, he tried to reach in his pants pocket again. When I blocked him, he fought with me in an attempt to run. After the suspect was secured, I found a penknife in his left pocket. I then found a piece of crack cocaine in the cigarette pack which the suspect threw earlier.[18]

The defendant pleaded guilty to possession of crack cocaine. The charges of battery on a law enforcement officer and resisting arrest with violence were dropped. The official report to the FBI, however, contained the more serious charges of "arrest with violence and battery of a law enforcement agent." In all likelihood, the prosecutor would not have been able to obtain a conviction given the police officer's report of what actually happened, but that makes no difference to the crime statistic, which neither corresponds to what the police officer reported nor reflects the real nature of the crime. Multiplying this case by the hundreds of thousands reported by local police to the FBI and "dutifully reported" in the *UCR* gives some idea of how grossly distorted are the crime statistics that form the basis for the media and public image of crime.

The FBI does not distinguish between attempted and completed crimes: "Generally, attempts to commit a crime are classified as though the crimes were actually completed. The only exception to this rule applies to attempted murder wherein the victim does not die."[19]

Most years the FBI and local police departments are under pressure to increase the reported number of crimes in order to support their budgetary requests for more personnel and more funding. Occasionally, however, there is political pressure to show a decrease in crime in order to show that the police are effectively controlling crime. A 1982 study of how the police in Indianapolis constructed crime rates found that the reported rates fluctuated according to whether those in political power wanted them to go up or down.[20]

The *UCR* includes theft of any object as a Type I, that is, very serious, crime. But since theft is by far the most common crime committed, including it drastically skews the crime rate. Here again, the FBI uses every trick available to exaggerate the extent and seriousness of the crime. Most jurisdictions distinguish between felony theft—which usually means the theft of something valued at more than $159.00—and misdemeanor theft. Not so the FBI, which defines felonious theft as "the unlawful taking, carrying, leading, or riding away of property from the possession or constructive possession of another." Since theft accounts for more criminal events than any other crime and since petty thefts are much more common than felony thefts, the FBI statistics grossly distort the reality.

Local police are not above manipulating the data to suit their own purposes. When Richard Nixon wanted to demonstrate that his War on Crime was effective,[21] the Washington, D.C., chief of police rallied his officers to lower the crime rate: "Either I have a man who will get the crime rate down in his district or I'll find a new man."[22] At the time, the city categorized theft of anything valued at more than fifty dollars as a felony. The next year, police officers began valuing the property in most reported thefts at $49.00 and did not report these to the FBI, even though the FBI's instructions said they should. Thus, Washington's official crime rate declined dramatically after the implementation of "get tough" policies. The chief "found the man" who would lower the crime rate, if not the crime incidence.

In New York in the 1990s Mayor Rudy Giuliani made a concerted effort to "clean up the city." He instructed the police commissioner to rid the streets of panhandlers, homeless people, and "squeegee men" (people who stand in the streets at intersections and offer to wash the windows of the cars stopped for the lights). That done, he instructed the commissioner to lower the crime rate and, voilà, the crime rate was lowered. Public opinion polls showed that people felt safer, and the mayor was given credit for reducing crime. Victim surveys, which give a much more reliable measure of changes in crime rates than do police statistics, showed no difference in the crime rate trends before and after the mayor's campaign. Politics, not any real difference in the amount of crime, changed the official crime rate reported by the police. Seeing the wonderful (political) results in New York, other cities quickly followed suit, and crime rates declined in Los Angeles, Houston, Chicago, and Detroit in the following years. That a decline in the crime rate would spread across the nation in an orderly fashion from one large city to the next is so unlikely that it defies logic.

Just as the police and prosecutor can escalate charges brought against suspects, they can also downgrade them. Burglary can become trespass; aggravated assault, simple assault; and even murder can be classified as "accidental death." Roland Chilton has shown that in New York during the years that Giuliani was taking credit for lowering the murder rate, deaths classified by the police as suicides went up by 40 percent at the same time that deaths reported by the police as homicides declined.[23]

Murder by Strangers

Faced with reports of lower violent crime rates, for the first time in decades, from police departments in some of the nation's largest cities, the FBI quickly attributed the lower crime rates to increased numbers of police officers and longer prison sentences. But these claims are belied by the facts. Victim surveys show that violent crime has been declining in the United States since 1973, long before the increase in the number of police officers, mandatory sentences, and longer prison sentences.

The FBI also attempts to counterbalance the good news of lower violent crime rates with data designed to sustain the fear of crime, namely, with data showing that (1) people are in more danger than ever of being victimized by strangers and (2) demographic changes in the most criminogenic population foretells a crime wave in the near future.

The FBI sent a news release to media outlets across the country in 1994 claiming that for the first time murders were more often committed by strangers than by acquaintances and that the percentage of murders committed by nonfamily members had increased:

> Historical statistics on relationships of victims to offenders showed that the majority of murder victims knew their killers. However, in the last few years (1991 through 1994) the relationship percentages

> have changed. In 1994, less than half of murder victims were related to (12 percent) or acquainted with (35 percent) their assailants. Thirteen percent of the victims were murdered by strangers, while the relationships among victims and offenders were unknown for 40 percent of the murders.[24]

The *Washington Post,* along with newspapers across the country, reported in a front-page article that the "number of people killed . . . by unknown persons has grown in the 1990s."[25]

The FBI news release and the media's knee-jerk parroting of the findings is a classic case of law enforcement propaganda masquerading as fact. The increase in "murders by strangers" is a statistical artifact accounted for in part by an increase in unsolved murders. Between 1991 and 1994 the number of murders for which the police made an arrest dropped by more than 5 percent compared to the preceding ten-year period.

A second reason for the apparent increase in the number of murders by strangers is an increase in murders resulting from "drive-by shootings." The police categorize these as murder by strangers. But because drive-by shootings are often the result of turf battles between competing gangs selling drugs, the chances are very good that the assailant and victim knew each other and that the victim knew his or her assailant well enough to be killed for competing or "snitching."

The FBI news release went on to state that "In 1965, nearly a third of the murders in this country were family related . . . [but by] 1992, a little more than one out of 10 of the nation's homicides were family related."[26] The *Washington Post* quoted Gilford S. Gee, a contributor to the *UCR,* who noted that "Criminologists and sociologists used to point to the fact that most murders were committed by family members or acquaintances. . . . That was indeed the case, but no longer."[27]

The *Post* accurately reported the data they received from the Justice Department. But the Justice Department failed to point out that the number of unmarried couples living together has increased dramatically in recent years: From 1980 to 1997 the figure increased more than 260 percent to more than 4 million such couples.[28] If a live-in boyfriend kills his partner, the FBI does not report it as murder by a family member, so the decline in murders by family members is explained by the fact that more people living together are not married. Furthermore, the proportion of unmarried couples living together is highest in the poorest social classes, which are also the demographic groups with the greatest likelihood of murder among family members.

Given the increase in drive-by murders and in the number of unmarried couples cohabiting, the FBI claim that acquaintance and family murders no longer constitute the majority of homicides is erroneous. FBI data show that in 1994, 47 percent of all murders were of family members or acquaintances. Assuming that the unsolved murders contain the same proportions, then the observation by criminologists and sociologists that most murders are committed by family members or acquaintances is as true today as it ever was.

Selective Reporting

Department of Justice reports commonly select years for comparison in order to show increases in crime. In the 1994 *Uniform Crime Reports*, for example, the FBI compared the homicide rates of 1991 and 1994 to show an increase in "stranger" homicides for the period. In fact, 1991 and 1994 were about the only two years the FBI could have compared that would show the increase in stranger homicides it sought.

The FBI news releases do not mention the fact that the category of *substantiated* stranger homicides—that is, the number of homicides where it was determined that the assailant was a stranger—has remained fairly constant. With little fluctuation through the years, the figure now stands at 15 percent, the same as 1980.[29] Since these data will not serve to increase public paranoia about crime, the FBI prefers to draw faulty conclusions about the nature of unknown murderers.

Teenage "Super Predators"

In addition to raising a false alarm about a dramatic increase in stranger murders, the FBI and local law enforcement agencies periodically point to an alleged dramatic increase in the number of crimes committed by juveniles. Citing FBI sources, *U.S. News and World Report* published a warning in 1967 that the nation was experiencing an "explosion in teenage crimes":

> Deep worry is developing among the nation's leaders over juvenile delinquency that seems to be getting out of hand across the United States. More youngsters are getting arrested every year—at lower ages and for more serious offenses. Many will be graduating into the ranks of a criminal army that is costing America billions of dollars a year.[30]

In 1970, *U.S. News and World Report* published a story claiming that "In Long Beach, Calif., Police Sgt. James D. Reed says that young thugs who 'stalk older people, like animals stalking their prey,' robbing and brutally beating their victims, want 'excitement and money in their pockets.'"[31] *Look* magazine disclosed in 1966 that "More and more youngsters are involved in burglary, auto theft, shoplifting, and a variety of lesser crimes."[32]

Panic over youth crime is as persistent in Western society as is worry about the stock market, but, like so many other alarms, it is based on political and law enforcement propaganda, not facts. In the late 1990s another spate of law enforcement-driven propaganda about the "time bomb" of juvenile crime blossomed. That campaign was closely linked to the creation of anxiety over the state of the family in the United States, where children were said to be growing up "fatherless, jobless, and godless," and dependent on "welfare Moms."[33]

The data for these years make a lie of these alarmist reports. In 1966, 21 percent of those arrested for violent crimes and 23 percent of those arrested for all offenses were under eighteen. In 1969 the percentages were 22 percent and 26 percent, respectively. Juveniles accounted for 23 percent of the violent crime arrests and 26 percent of all arrests in 1971 and 1973. On average, juveniles accounted for around 22 percent of violent crime arrests and one quarter of the arrests for all offenses from 1966 to 1973.[34] These data do not support police and FBI claims reported in the press that there has been a dramatic acceleration in juvenile crime in recent years.

In fact, there has been a slight decline in the percentage of juvenile arrests among total arrests since the 1960s and 1970s. In 1994, individuals under eighteen contributed to 19 percent of violent crime arrests and 19 percent of arrests for all offenses. Juvenile arrests accounted for under 20 percent of total arrests for both violent crimes and all offenses from the mid-1980s to the present.[35]

That the percentage of arrests accounted for by juveniles is less today than in the 1960s and 1970s is explained by demographics. Arrest rates are the best index we have of the extent of juvenile crime, and these data show that juvenile crime generally keeps pace with the number of juveniles in the population. In the 1960s and 1970s people under eighteen made up a larger percentage of the population than they did in the 1990s. In 1960, 35.7 percent of the population was younger than eighteen, and this proportion remained relatively stable over the next ten years, rising to 36.1 percent in 1966 and falling to 34.2 percent in 1970.[36] From 1980 to the 1998, the proportion of the population under eighteen held steady at about 26 percent of the population, substantially lower than two or three decades earlier.[37] Following these demographic changes, the distribution of arrests by age changed as well. Between 1971 and 1994 the percentage of adults arrested increased from 74.2 percent to 81.4 percent, reflecting the increase in the proportion of the population over eighteen.

Current Panics over Juvenile Crime

Although the number of juveniles arrested remained relatively stable over the 1990s, there has been an unending public diatribe about the increasing danger posed by juvenile crime.[38] The panic is fueled not just by law enforcement agencies but by publicity-seeking criminologists as well. They point to the "near future," when demographic changes will supposedly once again create a massive increase in juvenile crime.

Newsweek announced in 1995 that "Criminologists are already warning that the United States can expect another wave of violent crime in the coming decade, and some say it will be much worse than the one that is now subsiding."[39] *Time* magazine in 1996 warned that individuals between fourteen and seventeen, "the age group that in the early '90s supplanted 18-to–24 year-olds as the most crime prone . . . is precisely the age group that will be booming in the next decade."[40] These articles cite not only the FBI and local police but right-wing criminologists like John J. DiIulio Jr. of Princeton University, who warns that in the near future the nation will face a generation of "superpredator" teenagers. James Alan Fox, of Northeastern University, joins this chorus: "So long as we fool ourselves in thinking that we're winning the war against crime, we may be blindsided by this bloodbath of teenage violence that is lurking in the future."[41]

The Bureau of the Census, however, projects that the percentage of the population under eighteen will in fact decline, from 26.2 percent in 1996 to 25.9 percent by 2000 and to 23.6 percent by 2025. In 1996, 5.5 percent of the population was between fourteen and seventeen; and that percentage will decline to 5.3 by 2025. If the alarmists like Fox and DiIulio are correct in thinking that shifts in the size of the juvenile population affect violent crime rates, we should see a decline in violent crime over the next twenty-five years, not an increase.

Other criminologists support their predictions of a "bloodbath of teenage violence" by claiming there will be a dramatic increase in the number of minority teenagers. James Fox and Glenn Pierce maintain that "the amount of 15–19 year-olds will rise 28 percent among blacks and 47 percent among Hispanics."[42] But an increase in the number of teenagers among the black and Hispanic populations does not translate directly into an increase in violent crime. From 1980 to 1997 the black population between the ages of fifteen and thirty-four increased by 27 percent, but the overall violent crime rate for that age group did not experience an equivalent increase. For example, violent crime among urban juveniles, often one of the most violent sectors of the population, has decreased by 6.8 percent since 1995.[43]

Fox and Pierce also neglect to point out that the black and Hispanic population will make up only a minimally larger percentage of the total population: The percentage of African American youths from fourteen to twenty-four will increase from 2.3 percent of the population in 1995 to 2.4 percent in 2005. The percentage of Hispanics will increase slightly, from 1.9 percent to 2.3 percent.[44]

The Department of Justice also uses percentage increase statements to exaggerate crime and spread fear among the population. *Juvenile Offenders and Victims: A National Report*, prepared by the Office of Juvenile Justice and Delinquency Prevention (OJJDP), warns that "If trends continue as they have over the past 10 years, juvenile arrests for violent crime will double by the year 2010."[45] The report estimates that 261,000 juveniles will be arrested for violent crimes in 2010, a 101 percent increase from the 129,600 arrests for the same offenses in 1992. But this statistic has little practical meaning, since it is not placed in the context of all arrests. The number of adult arrests will also increase in the future because the total population continues to grow, expanding the pool of potential arrestees.

Furthermore, the OJJDP's dire prediction presumes that annual increases in juvenile arrests for violent crimes over the next fifteen years will mirror the annual increases in juvenile arrests for violent crimes that occurred between 1983 and 1992. However, recall that although the juvenile population has remained relatively stable at 26 percent of the population since 1980, the Census Bureau projects it will decrease to 24.6 percent by 2010. The Justice Department's assumption that juvenile arrests will keep pace with those of the past when the percent of the population under eighteen is declining reveals a desire to fuel public anxiety about a teenage "bloodbath."

Even more misleading are the OJJDP's statistics about arrest rates for juveniles. The report claims that "The increase in violent crime arrest rates is disproportionate for juveniles and young adults," and it presents six graphs showing juvenile arrests for violent offenses outdistancing adult arrests for the same categories.[46] These "facts" were then presented by the conservative Council on Crime in America, whose membership includes the right-wing criminologist John DiIulio, and published in 1996 under the title "The State of Violent Crime in America."[47]

To arrive at the conclusion that the juvenile violent crime rate is accelerating faster than the adult violent crime rate, the authors of *Juvenile Offenders and Victims* compared juvenile arrests per 100,000 people aged 10–17—*not,* as claimed in the title of the graph purporting to show the acceleration, per 100,000 total population. People under ten, the report tells us, were eliminated because they are rarely arrested. They calculated arrest rate for adults, however, based on a population of everyone over eighteen years of age. By the same logic that led to calculating the crime rate only for the 10–17 age group, the youth population most likely to be arrested, it would be necessary to also limit the adult arrest rate calculation to the age groups most likely to be arrested. At the very least, the 65+ age group should be eliminated because, like children under ten, people over sixty-five are very unlikely to be arrested. Even more interesting would be to compare the arrest rate of the 10–17 age group to that of the 18–35 age group, since this is the adult group in which most arrests occur. Once again, a U.S. Department of Justice report presents so-called research in a way designed to spread fear. The media and generously funded right-wing think tanks spread the news, insisting that

> Americans must search for better, more cost-effective ways of *preventing* violent crimes and *protecting* themselves and their loved ones from violent and repeat criminals, adult and juvenile. But our first order of business must be *restraining* known convicted, violent and repeat criminals. *Restraining violent criminals* is a necessary but insufficient condition for meeting America's crime challenges, reforming the justice system, and *restoring public trust* in the system and in representative democracy itself. [Emphasis in original][48]

Questionable math also underlies DiIulio's frequently made statement that the number of juvenile male "superpredators" will increase significantly in coming years. In an article with the dubiously accurate title "Crime in America: It's Going to Get Worse," DiIulio asserted that

> The current trend in birth rates makes it certain that a new violent crime wave is just around the corner. Today there are some 7.5 million males ages 14 through 17. By the year 2000 we will have an additional 500,000. About six percent of young males are responsible for half the serious crimes committed by their age group, studies reveal. Thus, in a few years we can expect at least 30,000 more murderers, rapists, robbers and muggers on the streets than we have today.[49]

DiIulio bases his conclusions on studies "that have shown about 6 percent of all boys are responsible for about half of all the police contacts with minors."[50] However, studies of this 6 percent group in several cities indicate that "almost no life-threatening violence showed up in the youth samples that were responsible for the majority of all police contacts . . . [and that] no study of any youth population supports [a] projection of predatory violence."[51]

DiIulio also argues that 270,000 superpredators will be added to the U.S. population by the year 2010. However, as Franklin Zimring pointed out, "If 6 percent of all males under 18 are superpredators, that means we currently have more than 1.9 million juvenile superpredators on our streets. We would hardly notice another 270,000 by 2010."[52] Moreover, DiIulio calculates the number of superpredators as a percentage of *all* males under eighteen. But "[s]ince 93 percent of all juvenile arrests for violence occur after age 13,"[53] very few violent crimes are committed by youths under the age of thirteen. To get a total of 270,000 potentially violent youths, DiIulio must include infants, toddlers, and little boys.

Currently there are 7,961,000 people from fourteen to seventeen years old in the population, and there will be 718,000 added to this cohort by the year 2010.[54] This is a substantial increase, but it is nowhere close to DiIulio's estimation. Furthermore, to assume that the proportion of "dangerous" young males is constant is ludicrous, since the factors that create violence cannot be reduced simply to a person's age. Even the FBI acknowledges that age is only one of the variables associated with an increased likelihood of violence.

School Violence

In the closing years of the twentieth century, schools became the venue of a number of shootings in which young people were killed and wounded. These apparently senseless attacks spawned a political, law enforcement, and media frenzy along with hordes of "experts" espousing psychobabble to explain why and what should be done about it. The end result was predictable: The general public panicked. The number of Americans expressing increased fear for the safety of their children in schools rose by fifty percent. Sixty percent of poll respondents said school safety worried them "a great deal."

Police and prosecutors fanned the flames with public statements and calls for metal detectors and police patrols in schools. The police department of Miami-Dade County in Florida had its antiterrorist squad call local high schools asking for the names of any students who might be dangerous or who were "Gothic." Prosecutors brought criminal charges for what would normally be considered a prank: Two ten-year-old boys in Arlington, Virginia, were charged with a felony and faced a possible twenty years in prison for putting soapy water into their teacher's drink. A boy in Ponchatoula, Louisiana, who warned his classmates not to eat all the potatoes or "I'm going to get you" was charged with making "terrorist threats" and incarcerated for two weeks while awaiting trial. In Denton County, Texas, a boy who completed an assignment to write a "scary" Halloween story was arrested and spent six days in jail for writing about shooting children in school.

The media went on a binge of stories and profiles of children who commit crimes, with an endless string of "experts" offering explanations and solutions.

What went practically unnoticed in this frenzy over school violence is that the rate of violence in schools was and is extremely low and has been declining for the past decade. Youth homicide arrests declined from 1993 to 1998 from 3,092 to 1,354. The total number of reported school crimes declined by 29 percent, and the number of serious violent crimes declined 34 percent. Schools are arguably the safest place in the country for children to spend time.

National Criminal Victimization Surveys

The distortion and manipulation of statistics by the Department of Justice is not limited to data collected by the FBI and local police departments. Even when data on crime are gathered objectively by the Census Bureau, the reports emanating from the Department of Justice's Bureau of Justice Statistics are constructed so as to maximize fear and minimize public understanding. The Bureau of Justice Statistics (BJS) is responsible for constructing the Census Bureau questionnaires and interpreting and reporting the findings. Once the data arrive in the BJS offices, they are under the control of a bureaucracy with a vested interest in presenting them in a particular light.

After pilot studies were conducted from 1967 to 1972, the first official National Criminal Victimization Survey (NCVS) appeared in 1973. Each year the survey asks a random sample of approximately 135,000 U.S. residents in 65,000 households whether they have been the victim of a crime during the past year.

Unlike the *Uniform Crime Reports,* the NCVS can register crimes not reported to or observed by the police. It also tallies all the crimes that occur in a particular incident, not just the most violent or "most serious." Like those of any survey instrument, the NCVS findings must be read cautiously. Residents of the highest-crime areas may be the least likely to be surveyed and the most reticent to accurately report their experiences. People may be reluctant to disclose their victimization. On the other side, faced with an interviewer probing to find victims of crime, respondents may well invent responses to fill out the interviewer's questionnaire or may inadvertently recount crimes that transpired more than a year earlier.

The main problem with the NCVS reports, however, is not that they have methodological weaknesses but that their results are creatively summarized to buttress the political and bureaucratic interests of the Department of Justice.

The Bureau of Justice Statistics publication "Criminal Victimization, General" (February 11, 2000) begins with the following statement:

> In 1998, U.S. residents age 12 or older experienced approximately 31.3 million crimes
>
> - 73% (22.9 million) were property crimes
> - 26% (8.1 million) were crimes of violence
> - 1% (.3 million) were personal thefts

These statements are extremely misleading and do more to alarm than to inform the reader. In a population of 265 million people, the fact that 31.3 million are the victims of some kind of crime (mostly petty crimes; see Tables I.1 and 2.1) is nothing to be alarmed about. It means that *over 85 percent of the population were not the victim of any type of crime*. Three-fourths of those who are victims of a crime are victims of property crimes. Most (77 percent) property crimes are theft of property, 22 percent of which are thefts under $50 and only 14 percent are over $250 (see Table 2.1). Forty percent of the victims of property crimes do not report them to the police because the item was recovered or they could not prove it was stolen.

Of the 8.1 million crimes of violence, over 70 percent were attempts or threats of violence, not completed acts of violence. A less politicized statement of the violent crime rate as revealed by the victim survey would read, "In 1998 fewer than 2 percent of the total population of the United States were the victims of a violent

TABLE 2.1 Value of Property Stolen as Percent of All Property Theft

Value	*Percent of All Property Thefts*
$50 or less	22%
$51–249	64%
$251 and over	14%

crime. Another 24 percent were the victims of threatened or attempted violence." A truly objective report would then go on to describe some typical examples of the types of violent crimes included in the category. If examples of "threats" or "attempts" were provided, it probably would undermine the thrust of the report, for in all likelihood it would reveal that what is being counted as "violent crime" consists of little more than arguments that do not culminate in any acts of physical violence.

Evidence for the fact that most of the crimes reported are not very serious comes from the respondents themselves. Almost 60 percent of the victims of completed, attempted, or threatened violent crimes do not report the crimes to the police. Why? Because they felt "the matter was private or personal in nature," they felt it was "not important enough," or they felt "nothing could be done about it."[55]

In almost every category of crime reported, *the least serious crime accounts for the majority of the instances reported.* In the NCVS the category "violent crimes" comprises rape, robbery, and assault (murder is not included, since the victims are not able to respond). Assault is the least serious of these, and assaults account for the vast majority (84 percent) of all violent crimes. Assault can be subdivided into aggravated and simple. Of the 9,128,000 assaults reported in 1994, 6,650,000 (73 percent) were simple assaults (with and without minor injury); the remaining 27 percent, 2,478,000 incidents, were aggravated assaults. Simple assault without injury—that is, "an attempted assault without a weapon not resulting in injury"—*accounts for nearly one half (48 percent) of all violent crimes.* Even victims of aggravated assaults rarely experience injuries: Among aggravated assaults less than one-third resulted in injury.

The systematic attempt to make the problem of crime seem as bad as the data will allow affects the reporting of property crimes as well. The report states: "In 1994 the NCVS measured 31 million household burglaries, motor vehicle thefts, and thefts of other property . . . Expressed as rates per 1,000 households, there were 54 burglaries, 18 motor vehicle thefts, and 236 property thefts."[56] As with violent crimes, these statements are not false, but they are clearly designed to maximize the seriousness of crime and the danger that crime poses for individuals. The fact is that the least serious of the property crimes, property theft, accounts for 77 percent of all property crimes, and thefts in which the property stolen is valued at less than $50.00 account for 22 percent of all victimizations. Only 14 percent of all property crimes reported by victims in 1994 were of property valued in excess of $250.00. More than 50 percent of property crime victims claimed they did not notify the police because (1) it was not serious enough, (2) nothing could be done about it, (3) the item was recovered, or (4) they could not prove it was stolen.[57]

The maxim that the least serious offense makes up the bulk of all offenses holds true within most categories of crime. Thus, in 1992, petty larceny (theft of property worth less than $100) without contact characterized 62.3 percent of the crimes of theft and 35 percent of all crimes. Petty larceny with contact accounted for 2.6 percent of all thefts and a minuscule 1.4 percent of the total number of crimes. Among household crimes, household larceny was responsible for 54.7 percent of the victimizations within the category, and burglary represented 32.1 percent of household crimes and only 14.1 percent of all crimes. Once again, the most serious crime, forcible entry burglary, is the least common type, representing only 10.8 percent of all household crimes and 4.8 percent of all victimizations.

What this analysis of the facts behind the NCVS report reveals is a systematic bias in summarizing the findings to make both the frequency and the seriousness of crime appear much worse than they really are. The NCVS's most consistent findings are that most crimes are not reported by the victim, that in almost every crime category surveyed the majority of the criminal victimizations are for the least serious offense in the category, and that there is no infliction of actual violence in the majority of so-called crimes of violence. Such data should lead the authors of the NCVS report to make highly-qualified, cautious statements about the extent to which there is a serious crime problem in the United States.

When the data are in the hands of the crime control industry, political and bureaucratic interests take priority over accuracy. Indeed, the opening statement of the NCVS report *could* say "Last year 85–90 percent of all residents in the United States were not the victims of any crime. Furthermore, the majority of those who were victimized were the victims of petty theft. Less than 1 percent of the population was the victim of any type of violent crime, and the vast majority of these victims were victims of attempted or threatened violence but suffered no actual violence."

The Consequences

If the politicization of crime statistics were merely a matter of one bureaucracy fiddling with data to support its own interests, perhaps we could ignore it as "good enough for government work." Unfortunately, when the subject is crime, the consequences of misreporting data reverberate in the lives of people throughout the country. The public image of crime in the United States is not racially neutral. The media and the general public see crime as acts committed by violent, psychopathic, young black males, even though serious crimes occur daily at corporate headquarters, in banks, and on Wall Street. Thus for the Department of Justice to distort the frequency and seriousness of crime is to accuse lower-class African Americans of being a dangerous class in need of massive control efforts.[58]

One consequence of this campaign to generate fear is to increase the gap between the white and black communities. People cross the street to avoid young black men. Mothers hurry to put their children in the car and lock the doors.

The quality of life *for everyone* is negatively affected as parents put fear into their children from an early age. Middle- and upper-class parents shuttle their children to and from the mall rather than letting them ride the bus or walk home after dark, even in neighborhoods that rarely experience any type of crime. Women's independence is severely curtailed: Afraid to walk alone, they become dependent on having a man escort them or on walking only in groups with other women.

One of the more important consequences of perpetuating the myth that crime is out of control is that it leads inevitably to the arrest and incarceration of the poor. Since African Americans are disproportionately poor in the United States the result is closely akin to "ethnic cleansing." In Washington, D.C., and Baltimore, Maryland, 40–50 percent of the black male population from eighteen to thirty-five are at any given moment either in prison, on probation or on parole, or has a warrant out for their arrest.[59] The consequences for the African American community are devastating. Young men cannot marry because they cannot find employment because they have a prison record. Children grow up knowing their father only through weekly visits to prison. Women with husbands in prison must work or go on welfare. If they find employment, they are forced to leave their children in the care of relatives or friends because they cannot afford day care. The perpetuation of this myth also justifies the elimination of support systems such as welfare and job-creation programs because the poor increasingly come to be defined as "the inherently criminal dangerous classes" and therefore "undeserving."[60]

Another consequence is the transformation of urban police departments into militarized, heavily armed tactical units whose mission is preemptive strikes and whose behavior makes a mockery of constitutional guarantees. Meanwhile the Supreme Court, itself a victim of the propaganda of the law enforcement–industrial complex, eats away at civilian protections from police misuse of power, allowing more and more incursions into private spaces such as automobiles and homes with fewer and fewer controls over police.

Finally, criminal justice budgets are growing at the expense of all other public expenditures. For the first time in history, state and municipal governments are spending more on criminal justice than on education.[61] Scarcely a politician can be found who will stand up and say, as did Lyndon Johnson, John Kennedy, and Hubert Humphrey, that the crime problem has to be solved by spending more money on education, opportunities, and job creation rather than on police, prosecutors, judges, and prisons.

Conclusion

The FBI's *Uniform Crime Reports* and the Department of Justice's National Criminal Victimization Surveys have lived up to the Wickersham Commission's worst fears with consequences for U.S.

citizens that could scarcely have been imagined sixty years ago. One consequence is the emergence of a crime control industry siphoning resources from other social services. Even more important, however, is the creation of law enforcement bureaucracies whose survival depends on making arrests and putting people in prison. This leads in turn to the arrest and conviction of the poor for minor offenses. It also institutionalizes the division of the United States into two hostile nations, "separate and unequal."

Notes

1. Department of Justice, *The Budget for Fiscal Year 1999, Historical Tables* (Washington, D.C.: GPO, 1988).
2. Bureau of Justice Statistics, *Sourcebook of Criminal Justice Statistics*, 1982 (Washington, D.C.: U.S. Department of Justice, 1983), and *Sourcebook of Criminal Justice Statistics*, 1996 (Washington, D.C.: U.S. Department of Justice, 1997).
3. National Association of State Budget Officers, *State Expenditure Report* (Washington, D.C., March 1994), 47.
4. Chris Bryson, "Crime Pays for Those in the Prison Business," *The National Times*, September 1996, 28–35.
5. Ibid.
6. Wickersham Commission, *Report on Criminal Statistics* (Washington, D.C.: GPO, 1931), 1.
7. Albert J. Meehan, "I Don't Prevent Crime, I Prevent Calls: Policing as a Negotiated Order," *Symbolic Interaction* 15, no. 4 (1992): 455–480.
8. Federal Bureau of Investigation, *Crime in the United States: Uniform Crime Reports* (Washington, D.C.: U.S. Department of Justice, 1998), 4. Further references in this chapter to this annual publication will be to *UCR*, identified by the relevant year.
9. *UCR*, 1984, 40.
10. *UCR*, 1998, 14.
11. Ibid., 22.
12. Ibid.
13. Federal Bureau of Investigation, *Uniform Crime Reporting Handbook* (Washington, D.C.: U.S. Department of Justice, 1984), 6.
14. *UCR*, 1981.
15. Harry J. Subin, *The Criminal Process: Prosecution and Defense Functions* (West, 1993).
16. Committee on the Judiciary, 103rd Cong., 1st sess., July 29, 1993.

17. Federal Bureau of Investigation, *Uniform Crime Reporting Handbook* (Washington, D.C.: Federal Bureau of Investigation, 1984), 6.

18. William J. Chambliss and Barry Holman, "Creating Crime" (paper delivered at the American Society of Criminology Meetings, November 1994).

19. *UCR*, 1984, 33.

20. Harold Pepinsky and William Selke, "The Politics of Police Reporting in Indianapolis, 1948–1978," *Law and Human Behavior* 6 (1982): 47–61.

21. David Seidman and Michael Couzens, "Getting the Crime Rate Down: Political Pressure and Crime Reporting," *Law and Society Review* 8 (1974): 457–493.

22. Ibid., 482.

23. William J. Chambliss and Roland Chilton, "Fluctuations in Crime Rates: Artifact or Substance?" (paper delivered at the Society for the Study of Social Problems, San Francisco, August 1998).

24. Federal Bureau of Investigation, "Stranger Homicides" (Washington D.C.: FBI National Press Office, 1995).

25. Pierre Thomas, "The New Face of Murder in America: Family Slayings Decline; Fewer Cases Are Solved; Killers Are Younger," *Washington Post*, October 23, 1995, A4.

26. Ibid.

27. Ibid.

28. Bureau of the Census, *Statistical Abstract of the United States* (Washington, D.C.: U.S. Department of Commerce, 1998).

29. Federal Bureau of Investigation (1997), 17.

30. "Why Streets Are Not Safe," *U.S. News and World Report*, March 16, 1967, 74.

31. *U.S. News and World Report* (1970).

32. J. Robert Moskin, "The Suburbs Made to Order for Crime," *Look*, May 31, 1966, 24.

33. Richard Zoglin, "Now for the Bad News: A Teenage Time Bomb," *Time*, January 15, 1996, 52.

34. *UCR*, 1967, 1970, 1974, 1989.

35. *UCR*, 1984, 1986, 1988, 1990, 1992, 1998.

36. Bureau of the Census, *Statistical Abstract of the United States*.

37. Ibid.

38. See Albert J. Meehan, "The Organizational Career of a Statistic: Gang Statistics and the Politics of Policing Gangs," report to Office of Juvenile Justice and Delinquency Prevention, 1998, 1–46.

39. William Morganthau, "The Lull Before the Storm?" *Newsweek*, December 14, 1995, 42.

40. Zoglin, "Now for the Bad News," 52.

41. Both quoted in ibid.

42. James Allen Fox and G. Pierce, "American Killers Are Getting Younger," *USA Today Magazine,* January 1994, 26.

43. *UCR,* 1997.

44. Bureau of the Census, *Statistical Abstract of the United States.*

45. Howard N. Snyder and Melissa Sickmund. *Juvenile Offenders and Victims: A National Report* (Washington, D.C.: U.S. Department of Justice, 1997), 111.

46. Ibid.

47. Council on Crime in America, *The State of Violent Crime in America* (Washington, D.C.: The New Citizen Project, January 1996).

48. John J. DiIulio Jr., "Crime in America: It's Going to Get Worse," *Reader's Digest,* August 1995, 57.

49. Ibid.

50. Franklin E. Zimring, "Crying Wolf over Teen Demons," *Los Angeles Times,* August 19, 1996, 12.

51. Ibid.

52. Ibid.

53. Ibid.

54. Bureau of Census, *Statistical Abstract of the United States,* 17.

55. Bureau of Justice Statistics, "Criminal Victimization, General," Washington, DC., U.S. Department of Justice, February 11, 2000, p. 1); Bureau of Justice Statistics, *Sourcebook of Criminal Justice Statistics,* 1982–1999 (Washington, D.C.: U.S. Department of Justice, 2000).

56. Craig Perkins and Patsy Klaus, *Criminal Victimization in the United States, 1994* (Washington, D.C.: U.S. Department of Justice, 1996), 2–3.

57. Craig Perkins, Patsy Klaus, Lisa Bastian, and Robin Cohen, *Criminal Victimization in the United States, 1994* (Washington, D.C.: U.S. Department of Justice, 1996).

58. William J. Chambliss, "Policing the Ghetto Underclass: The Politics of Law and Law Enforcement," *Social Problems* 41, no. 2 (1994): 77–194.

59. M. Maurer, *Americans Behind Bars: The International Use of Incarceration, 1992–1993* (Washington, D.C.: The Sentencing Project, 1994); Jerome G. Miller, *Hobbling a Generation: Young African American Males in Washington D.C.'s Criminal Justice System* (Alexandria Va.: National Center on Institution and Alternatives, April 1992).

60. Herbert J. Gans, *The War Against the Poor: The Underclass and Antipoverty Policy* (New York: Basic Books, 1995).

61. William J. Chambliss, *Trading Textbooks for Prison Cells* (Alexandria, Va.: National Center on Institution and Alternatives, 1992), 1–17.

Part 2

Practice

Chapter Three

Finding Crime I: The Ghetto

Convincing the American people that they should be panicked over crime has led to the most rapid increase in the number of police, prosecutors, and prison inmates in history. But the crime control industry is not focused equally. The poor, especially urban poor African Americans, are disproportionately the subjects of law enforcement activities at all levels, from arrest to imprisonment. (See Table 3.1.)[1] The urban poor minorities are stereotyped as inherently criminogenic. Their high rates of crime are blamed on everything from their genes to the high percentage of female-headed households, teenage mothers, and welfare dependents in minority communities to the prevalence of youth gangs.

Crime in the ghetto is a self-fulfilling prophesy. Because the police target the urban ghettos for intensive surveillance, it is the residents of the urban ghettos who appear over and over again in the revolving door of jails, courts, and prisons. To understand how this process works, my students and I have logged more than a hundred hours since the early 1990s riding in police cars and observing the routine activities of police officers as they confront suspects and make arrests. The analysis that follows is based on the carefully recorded field notes of our observations and descriptions of policing the ghetto.

TABLE 3.1 Percentage of Arrests and Prison Population by Race and Ethnicity, 1998

	% of Population	% of Arrests	% of State Prison Population
White non-Hispanic	74	66.8	41.6
Minorities	26	31.2	56.7
African American	13	30.9	41.1
Hispanic	8	N/A[a]	15.6
American Indian	1.1	1.1	0.7

SOURCE: Kathleen Maguire and Ann L. Pastore, eds., *Sourcebook of Criminal Justice Statistics, 1997* (Washington, D.C.: U.S. Department of Justice, Bureau of Justice Statistics, 1998), 178.

[a] Not available.

The Dirty Harrys

In response to the urban riots of the 1960s, Washington, D.C., like many other cities, established a specialized riot control unit, the Rapid Deployment Unit (RDU). Approximately 10 percent of all municipal law enforcement personnel are now employed in specialized police units like Washington's RDU. Such specialized units account for 25 percent of police departments' budgets. These specialized units are trained to respond quickly and with force to the threat of riots or urban disturbances. Even in the United States, riots do not happen that often. For these specialized riot units, the War on Drugs provides an alternative raison d'être.

My students and I spent much of our time with members of the RDU. The RDU is known in the department as the "Dirty Harrys" and as "very serious bad-ass individuals." It is deployed in teams of three patrol cars with two officers in each car. Though the cars may cover different routes, they are never so far from one another that they cannot quickly converge in one place when summoned. They patrol the urban ghetto: the area of the city occupied by poor African American and Latino populations.

The RDU organizes its efforts at crime control around three distinct activities: the "rip," vehicular stops, and serving warrants.

The Rip

In the "rip," undercover agents buy drugs to identify the person selling them. Obviously undercover agents must maintain their cover, which makes the process somewhat complicated. How can undercover agents identify their sources to uniformed officers without revealing their identity as undercover agents? The following excerpt from our field notes illustrates how it is done:

RIPS: CASE 1

It is about 1730 hours on a hot summer day in 1992. RDU is patrolling the Seventh District. The Seventh District police are doing drug raids called "rips." An undercover officer approaches a person suspected of dealing drugs and makes a buy of $10.00 worth of crack cocaine. The officer then walks away. Another undercover officer is watching. The second officer radios uniformed officers and gives a brief description of the offender. The uniformed officers move in and arrest the suspect. The suspect is then taken to a remote street corner where he is photographed and told to look out into traffic. Various cars drive by. One of the cars is being driven by the officer who made the buy. He looks at the apprehended suspect and positively identifies him.

The purpose of this elaborate process is to maintain the secret identity of the undercover officers. If suspects were arrested immediately, officers would be compromised in the community. If necessary they will testify later in court, but since these cases almost inevitably end in guilty pleas, the officers' testimony is usually not needed and they can continue as undercover agents.

Most "rips" do not go as smoothly as the one just described. Suspects often flee or enter a building before the uniformed police can make an arrest.

RIPS: CASE 2

It is 10:25 at night when an undercover agent purchases $50.00 of crack cocaine from a young black male. The agent calls us and tells us that the suspect has just entered a building and gone into an apartment. We go immediately to the apartment, the police enter without warning with their guns drawn. Small children begin to scream and cry. The adults in the apartment are thrown to the floor, the police are shouting, the three women in the apartment are swearing and shouting "You can't just barge in here like this . . . where is your goddam warrant?" The suspect is caught and brought outside. The identification is made and the suspect is arrested. The suspect is sixteen years old.

While the suspect is being questioned one policeman says, "I should kick your little black ass right here for dealing that shit. You are a worthless little scumbag, do your realize that?"

Another officer asks, "What is your mother's name, son? My mistake . . . she is probably a whore and you are just a ghetto bastard. Am I right?"

The suspect is cooperative and soft-spoken. He does not appear to be menacing or a threat. He offers no resistance to the police. It seems that the suspect's demeanor is causing the police officers to become more abusive verbally. The suspect is handled very roughly. Handcuffs are cinched tightly, and he is shoved against the patrol car. His head hits the door frame of the car as he is pushed into the back seat of the patrol car. One of the officers comments that it is nice to make "a clean arrest."

[The arresting officer was asked whether or not it is legal to enter a home without a warrant.] "This is Southeast [Washington] and the Supreme Court has little regard for little shit like busting in on someone who just committed a crime involving drugs . . . Who will argue for the juvenile in this case? No one can and no one will."

RIPS: CASE 3

[A "rip" is made involving an older (thirty-four years old) black male.]

It is after midnight and the suspect enters a local strip bar. Three patrol cars race up the street and jump the curb to block the entrance. In the process one officer on foot who is nearly hit by a patrol car jumps and tears up his knee on the wet pavement. Three patrol cars surround the front of the establishment. The arrest team charges in the front door with their weapons drawn. The officers retrieve the suspect and drag him out to the hood of the patrol car. The suspect might have walked of his own volition but is never given the opportunity. The suspect denies any wrongdoing and becomes upset and

> confused by the arrest. He appears to be slightly intoxicated or high on drugs. He is forced to sit down on the front bumper of one of the patrol cars. He is instructed to sit on his handcuffed hands with his legs crossed.
>
> The suspect says, "What is this shit? This is all a bunch of bullshit, man. You guys don't got shit on me, man. Kiss my ass."
>
> One of the officers responds by forcefully shoving the suspect against the grill of the car. The officer places his flashlight against the side of the suspect's face and presses it hard into the suspect's cheek [and says] "Listen shorty, you say one more word and that's your hospital word. I will lay you out in a heartbeat so shut your damn mouth."

Rips account for approximately one-third of the arrests made by the RDU. In a large percentage of rips, the person approached by the undercover agent does not possess any drugs when initially approached. He or she will tell the agent to wait for a few minutes, go into a building or around a corner, and return with the requested amount of drugs. These cases raise the question of whether the person selling the drugs is in reality a drug dealer or merely someone taking advantage of an unexpected opportunity. Interviews with a number of people arrested in rips suggest that many of them are the latter: They were approached by someone wanting drugs, saw an opportunity to make a few dollars as a middleman, and ended up being arrested as a drug dealer.

There is another consequence of rips that has escaped public attention: The undercover officers cannot function in the community of drug dealers without themselves taking drugs. In some instances taking drugs is as pleasant for the officer as it is for other drug users, and he or she ends up taking bribes or cooperating with drug dealers in order to maintain a supply of drugs.

Vehicular Stops

The inequitable enforcement of motor vehicle regulations, in which disproportionately many black drivers are stopped for suspected violations, has long been a contentious issue. In the black community there is even a term for what is not legally a crime: "DWB," or "driving while black." Congressman John Conyers, who represents a primarily black constituency of Michigan, succeeded in getting a bill (H.R. 118) passed requiring that records be kept of the reason for a stop and the race of the persons stopped for suspected vehicular violations. The wording of the bill is self-explanatory: "The offense of 'D.W.B.' or 'driving while black' is well-known to African-American males across the country. There are virtually no African-American males—including Congressmen, actors, athletes, and office workers—who have not been stopped at one time or another for an alleged traffic violation, namely driving while black."

Approximately 50 percent of the arrests made by members of the RDU in Washington come from vehicular stops. RDU units patrol the ghetto continuously looking for cars with young black men in them. They are especially attentive to newer-model cars—Isuzu four-wheel-drive vehicles, BMWs, and Honda Accords—believing that these are the favorite cars of drug dealers. During the time of my observations, however, the RDU officers came to the conclusion that drug dealers were leaving their fancy cars at home in order to avoid vehicular stops. It thus became commonplace for them to stop any car with young black men in it.

In a nod to legality, the officers look for a violation in order to justify a vehicular stop: "As we pass a new-looking BMW with two black men in it the driver of the patrol car says to his partner, 'Joe, check out that car for violations.' The partner says quickly, 'Broken tail light, hit the horn.' The siren is put on and the car pulls over" (field notes). Any minor infraction is an excuse: going through a yellow light, not stopping completely at a stop sign, having something hanging from the rearview mirror (a violation almost every car in the southeast section of the city is guilty of). In addition, I was told "confidentially" by some of the officers (though neither I nor any of my students ever observed it) that if the officers felt strongly that they should stop a car they would pull the car over and break a taillight as they approached: "This is the jungle . . . we rewrite the Constitution every day down here . . . If we pull everyone over they will eventually learn that we aren't playing games any more. We are real serious about getting the crap off the streets" (field notes). Once a car is stopped the officers radio for backup. The two other cars in the area immediately come to the scene and triangulate the suspect's car: One car pulls in close behind and the two other cars form a V in front of the suspect's car.

Vehicular stops occur on an average of every twenty minutes throughout the shift. From our observations, the officers find illegal drugs, guns, weapons, or someone with an outstanding arrest warrant in only 10 percent of the stops. The officers themselves believe that they find serious violations in "about a third" of the vehicular stops. The following cases are typical vehicular stops:

VEHICULAR STOPS: CASE 1

12:15 A.M. A car is spotted with a broken headlight. The patrol car pulls over the vehicle and runs the license plate number through the computer. One officer approaches the vehicle from the rear and another approaches on the opposite side of the car. Both officers have their Glocks [guns] drawn. Momentarily the car is surrounded by two other patrol cars triangulating the stopped car.

One officer goes to the window of the car and says, "Good evening. My name is officer ———. I am with the Rapid Deployment Unit. Our job is to remove guns and drugs from the streets. Do you have any guns or drugs on your person or inside the vehicle?"

The driver of the car says there are none. The officer requests permission to search the car. The individual refuses the officers' request. The officer begins pressuring the driver with threats: "You know what happens if you refuse to obey a police officer's request?"

The driver says nothing, shrugs, and gets out of the car. The car is searched and nothing is found. A check is made for outstanding warrants of everyone in the car. There are none. The suspects are released with a warning to "never let me catch you with anything, you understand?"

VEHICULAR STOPS: CASE 2

After midnight. The driver of the patrol car points out a car driven by two young black men. He tells his partner to check for violations. The partner says, "pull 'em over. Broken taillight."

The officers call for backup. Two other RDU patrol cars arrive, and the suspects' car is surrounded by the three cars. Two officers approach the car on each side. The driver rolls down his window and the officer asks to see his license, which is given without comment. The officer on the other side of the car asks to see some identification of the passenger and is given his driver's license. The licenses are given to a third officer who removes himself to his car to check for warrants and to check the license plate of the car.

The officer on the driver's side asks, "Can we search your car?"

The driver says, "No."

The officer then says, "You know what will happen if you refuse a police officer's request?"

The driver then says, "OK, you can look."

Both occupants are told to get out of the car and the car is searched. The officers find nothing.

Apparently satisfied that there are no drugs or guns in the car, the officer says, "OK. You can go; but don't let us catch you with any shit, you understand?" The driver nods yes, everyone returns to their cars.

VEHICULAR STOPS: CASE 3

Another vehicular stop takes place at 12:17 [A.M.] that follows the same pattern. Again there are two black men in the car. This time the officers approach the car with their guns drawn and tell the occupants to get out of the car. One officer points to a small piece of white paper on the back seat. The driver of the car is extremely nervous. He keeps putting his hands into his pockets, then pulling them out. He seems to be trying to push his hand through his pants pockets.

"What's in your pants?"

The driver responds, "Nothin', man, Nothin'."

Officer: "Empty pockets, quick."

The driver seems confused but complies. An envelope containing perhaps two grams of crack cocaine is handed to the officer, who opens the packet, smirks, and tells the driver to put his hands on the top of the car. The officer on the other side of the car follows suit. Both men are handcuffed and taken to the patrol car. No one says anything.

Search Warrants

The third main activity of the RDU is carrying out search warrants, issued by a court based on information received from informants, undercover agents, or observations, to search an apartment or home.

VEHICULAR STOPS: CASE 4

9:15 P.M. A rusted 1978 Bonneville Pontiac is spotted and the officer witnesses the vehicle making erratic lane changes. The officer follows at a distance of about 100 yards. The vehicle attempts to go through a yellow light, which turns red before the vehicle gets through the intersection. The officer hits his siren and pulls the car over. He calls in the license plate number and advances to the driver's side of the car. He has no other officer with him, only the observer. His gun is not drawn. The officer notifies the driver of the offense and he begins to search the car visually. The suspect is asked, "Can I search your car?" The suspect says yes, but the officer declines the offer. The suspect is written up for running a red light, is told to have a good evening, and is released.

Observations of routine practices when carrying out a warrant show similar differences in police procedures in the predominantly white section of Washington.

WARRANT: CASE 1

Five RDU officers enter an apartment about 10:45 P.M. Before entering the officers draw their guns; they break down the door and rush in. The suspect is spotted, guns are pointed at him and he is told to "lie down, NOW." The suspect is handcuffed and taken outside. An elderly woman begins screaming and crying. She tells the officers to put their guns away. An officer goes to her, his gun still drawn, and tells her to "shut up or I'll pop you in the jaw." He physically forces her to lie down on the floor face down. The officers leave the apartment, put the suspect in the car and take him to the precinct for booking.

The RDU does not patrol the predominantly white sections of Washington. Observations of policing in this area of the city reveal an entirely different approach by the police. There are no rips, and no vehicular stops unless the driver has clearly committed a violation. Officers are not looking for cars with black drivers. If a car is stopped, other cars are not called as backups; the officer handles the infraction alone.

WARRANT: CASE 2

A warrant is issued by the court for the arrest of a suspected drug dealer wanted for assault and attempted murder. The Third District police are in an excited state over the pending arrest. An anonymous tip has provided them with information as to the suspect's whereabouts, and a discussion at the station lays out a plan for making the arrest. Twelve officers are dispatched to the house where the suspect is supposedly living. Seven officers surround the house and five others approach the front door. Most, but not all, of the officers have their guns drawn. In the dark it is not possible to see all of the officers, but of those observable three have guns drawn and two do not. It is a few minutes past 1 A.M. when the officers approach the front door. The doorbell is rung and the team leader shouts, "Police, open up." Everyone appears to be on edge. There is no response to the knock or the command. The officers break open the door. Flashlights are shining in every corner, behind furniture, and into people's eyes. A terrified elderly woman stands at the top of the stairs and asks what is going on. One of the officers approaches her with calmness and no gun drawn, speaks to her in a low voice, and gently removes her from the house to be watched by the team outside. The suspect is found in the basement behind a water cooler. He is identified and handcuffed. As he is being led from the house one officer says to him, "You sure have a pretty face, buddy boy. See you at the country club."

Routine Stops

Rips, warrants, and vehicular stops account for most of the confrontations between police and ghetto residents. A significant number, however, develop out of routine encounters between police officers and people, mostly young black males, on the streets.

For example, James Crane, a white police lieutenant with the District of Columbia Metropolitan Police, received a call on the police radio in his marked patrol car that guns were being fired near his location. He drove to the area, pulled his car alongside a young black man, and asked, "Did you hear any gunshots?" The young man stared at Crane and walked away. Crane got out of his car and walked toward the man, who began running. Crane and two other police officers chased him through an alley. The young man made it to his apartment and ran inside, locking the door behind him. The officers knocked on the door. The young man opened the door and yelled, "You have no reason to stop me." Lieutenant Crane tried to handcuff him, and he resisted. The lieutenant broke a fingernail, and the young man was bleeding from a scrape on the face.

A search of the house followed. Nothing illegal was found in the house or on the young man. Nonetheless, he was arrested and charged with a felony. According to Lieutenant Crane, the young man "had technically committed the crime of assault on a police officer. Although he had not attacked me, he had run away and resisted my attempts to question him."

At the station the young man told police that he worked every day, had never been in trouble, and was tired of being stopped by the police. He said that when he saw Crane in the police car he thought Crane was a "skinhead cop who was going to kick my ass just for being black." So he ran.

The next day, after consultation with the prosecutor, the charges were dropped—not because the entire incident had been caused by the police but because the prosecutor felt the evidence was not sufficient to get a conviction. The prosecutor said, "Well, Crane, you weren't assaulted and he didn't attack you, so we don't have much, do we?" Even though the charges were dropped, however, a young man with no prior record now has an arrest record, his fingerprints are now on file with the FBI, and his name has been entered into the National Crime Information Center's database.

On the other hand, as Lieutenant Crane said, "I came away from the incident with another arrest booked to my badge number and two hours of comp time for the time I spent at the court."[2] This arrest will reflect well on Lieutenant Crane's ability as a police officer and will improve his annual evaluation. But when the young man applies for a job or if he ever gets stopped again by the police, his arrest record is a serious blemish, which was manufactured by a suspicious police officer.

The Consequences

The young man whom Lieutenant Crane arrested ran because he was afraid of the police. His grandmother told Crane that her grandson "was probably right" to run away from police officers. Crane asked her, "Ma'am, you think I'm a racist who wanted to beat your grandson?" She replied, "I don't know you. You could be." She added that she "knew many young people in the District who are scared of police officers."[3]

Arrests and convictions for the possession and sale of drugs account for most of the astronomical increase in the number of African American men and women under the control of the criminal justice system (see Chapter 2). Thirty percent of all state prisoners and almost 60 percent of all federal prisoners in 1997 were convicted on drug violations.[4] Of all drug-related arrests in 1997, 80 percent were for possession of drugs; the rest (20 percent) were for their sale or manufacture.[5] More than 37 percent of all those arrested for drug-related violations were African Americans.[6] Yet the reality of drug use in the United States is that whites are two to three times as likely as blacks to use all illegal drugs except marijuana. Thus, more whites than blacks use illegal drugs, and more than 70 percent of the population is white. But 66 percent of the inmates in prison convicted of drug offenses are black, and only 33 percent are white or Hispanic.[7]

Arrests and convictions for the possession and sale of drugs account for most of the astronomical increase in the number of African American men and women under the control of the criminal justice system (see Chapter 4, Figure 4.1). Approximately 35 percent of all state prisoners and 60 percent of all federal prisoners in 1999 were convicted of drug violations. Of all drug-related arrests in 1999, 80 percent was for possession of drugs; the rest (20 percent) was for their sale or manufacture. African Americans

TABLE 3.2 Percentage of High School 12th-Grade Students Reporting Drug Use by Race and Ethnicity, 1997

	White	*Black*	*Hispanic*
Marijuana Use, Lifetime	41.0	34.0	39.0
Marijuana Use, Annual	34.0	26.0	17.0
Cocaine Use, Lifetime	6.0	1.5	9.4
Cocaine Use, Annual	4.0	1.0	5.5
Crack cocaine, Lifetime	2.9	1.3	4.7
Crack cocaine, Annual	1.9	1.0	3.1
Illegal Steroid use, lifetime	3.8	1.6	4.7
Other Illegal drug use, lifetime	18.4	3.9	18.1

SOURCE: Lloyd D. Johnston, Patrick M. O'Malley, and Jerald G. Bachman, *National Survey Results on Drug Use:* The Monitoring the Future Study, *1975–1998* (Washington, D.C.: National Institute on Drug Abuse, U.S. Department of Health and Human Services, 1999); Kathleen Maguire and Ann L. Pastore, eds., *Sourcebook of Criminal Justice Statistics* (Washington, D.C.: U.S. Department of Justice, Bureau of Justice Statistics, 1998).

represented nearly 40 percent of all those arrested for drug-related violations. If the current rate of incarceration of African Americans continues, by the year 2020 63 percent of all African American men between the ages of eighteen and thirty-four will be incarcerated, mainly for minor offenses (see Figure 3.1).

The variable severity of sentences for crimes involving different types of drugs is another manifestation of systematic racism in the criminal justice system. Jesse Helms (whose most recent campaign for senator was riddled with racist overtones) introduced an amendment that made the sentences for the possession of crack cocaine a hundred times more severe than the sentences for possession of powder cocaine. Helms's amendment provided for a mandatory sentence of five years in prison for possession of five grams of crack, which is nothing more than powder cocaine that has been heated with baking soda. For powder cocaine, a judge is only required to give a mandatory five-year sentence for possession of more than one hundred grams; for possession of less a person may receive probation or thirty days in jail. In the images of drug use generated in the popular media, crack is associated with African Americans and cocaine with white Americans, although the reality of drug use does not support this stereotype. (See Figure 3.2, Table 3.2.)

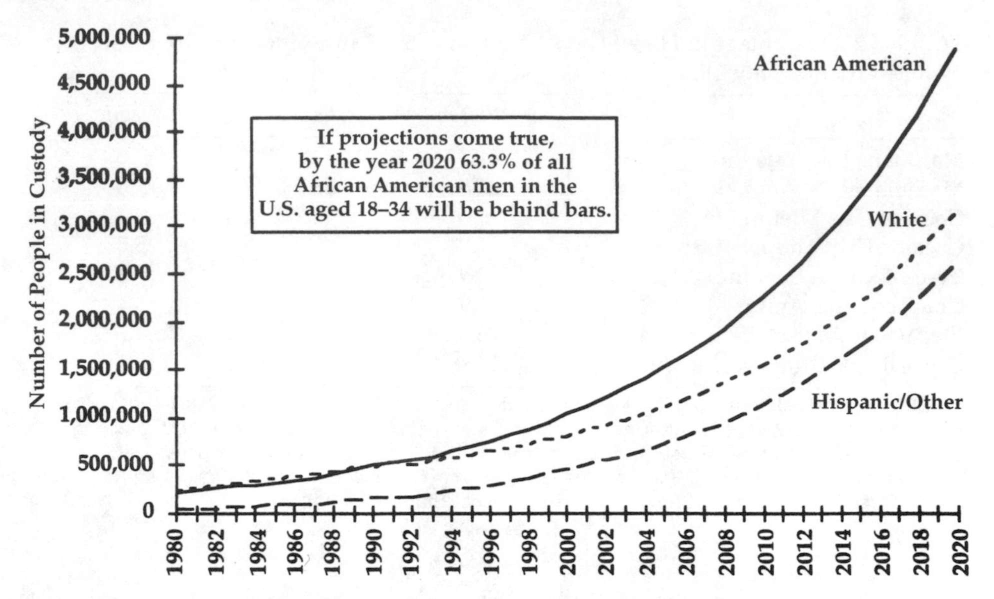

FIGURE 3.1 2020 Projections for Persons in Custody by Race/Ethnicity

SOURCE: Projected from data in Kathleen Maguire and Ann G. Pastore, *Sourcebook of Criminal Justice Statistics* (Washington, D.C.: U.S. Department of Justice. Bureau of Justice Statistics, 1999).

The Impact on the African American Community

The racism of the law and of law enforcement has not gone unnoticed in the black community. The intensive surveillance of black neighborhoods, the corresponding looseness of surveillance of white neighborhoods, and differences in punishments for white and black offenders reinforce the belief that the system is not only inherently racist but is designed to oppress, if not effectively commit genocide against, black people.

The law and law enforcement practices are major factors contributing to the ghettoization of the African American community and to the creation of an intractable class of abjectly poor. Any possibility that may otherwise have existed for normal families and a cohesive community is destroyed as the heart of the community is ripped out by the humiliation and degradation that law and law enforcement practices inflict on its young men and women. Young African American and Latino men are defined as a criminal group, arrested for minor offenses over and over again, given criminal records that justify and at times legally require man-

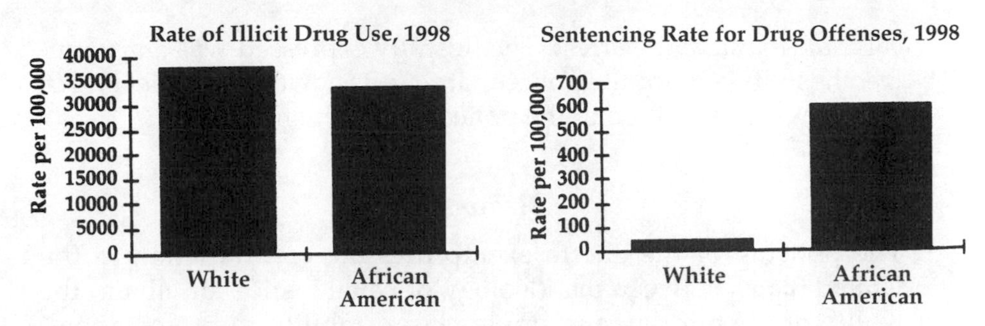

FIGURE 3.2 Racial Disparity in the War on Drugs

SOURCE: U.S. Department of Health and Human Serives, *National Household Survey on Drug Abuse.* U.S. Department of Justice, Bureau of Justice Statistics, 1999).

NOTE: "Use" is defined as whether the individual has *ever used* an illicit drug.

datory, long prison sentences. In a classic example of a self-fulfilling prophesy, the culture of the black community and the black family is then blamed for high rates of illegitimate children and unemployment.[8]

The overpolicing of the ghetto undermines the legitimacy of the police and makes law enforcement more difficult. Police complain that witnesses are not forthcoming even for serious, violent crimes and that community support is minimal. Blacks much more than whites believe that the police engage in verbal and physical abuse, are prejudiced against minorities, and routinely discriminate against minorities.[9] Twice as many blacks as whites say that they or someone in their family has been the victim of police brutality.[10]

On several occasions while riding with police officers, I and my students observed ghetto residents' hostility toward the police manifested in overt attacks and disruptive behavior. On one occasion police pursuing a car for speeding stopped the car in a cul-de-sac. People sitting on their front porches began pummeling the police with rocks, kitchen utensils, and even children's toys. On another occasion when police were arresting a man outside a convenience store, a crowd gathered and tried to free him. Someone in a nearby building began firing a pistol. It was not clear whether the shots were intended to hit anyone, but they were clearly intended to prevent the police from making the arrest. In neither of these instances did the people opposing the police know the men being arrested; nor were the police being brutal or even using much physical force to make the arrest. The hostility expressed was a generalized hostility toward the police that reflects a widespread feeling in the black community that the police are the enemy.

Discussion

The policing of the ghetto exemplifies the contradiction in the United States between the ideology of equal justice for all and the reality of the middle- and upper-classes' ability to protect themselves from being closely scrutinized by the police. To be perceived as effective and useful, the police must operate in a narrow space. A police officer's career and even annual income is determined by the number of "good collars"—that is, arrests that culminate in conviction—he or she makes. From the perspective of the police, the more serious the offense the better. A stream of politicians have defined drug use as a serious crime, drug arrests are among the easiest to make, convictions not too difficult to obtain, and drug convictions often lead to the longest prison terms (the average length of time served in state and federal prison for drug offenses is almost seven years).

An arrest is organizationally effective only if the person arrested is relatively powerless. Arrests of white male middle-class offenders (on college campuses, for example, or in the law offices of Wall Street) are guaranteed to cause the organization and the arresting officers strain because people with political influence or money hire attorneys to defend them. Arrests of poor black men, however, result in nothing but gains for the organization and the officer because the cases are quickly processed through the courts, a guilty plea is obtained, and the suspect is sentenced. Organizations reward members whose behavior maximizes gains and minimizes strains for the organization. In a class society, the powerless, the poor, and those who fit the public stereotype of "the criminal" are the human resources needed by law enforcement agencies to maximize gains and minimize strains. It is not surprising (though it is sociologically predictable), then, that vastly increasing the number of police officers in the last ten years has quadrupled the number of people incarcerated and has dramatically increased the percentage of inmates who are minorities. Furthermore, racist beliefs that make being a poor, young, black male, for all practical purposes, synonymous with being a criminal have become institutionalized.

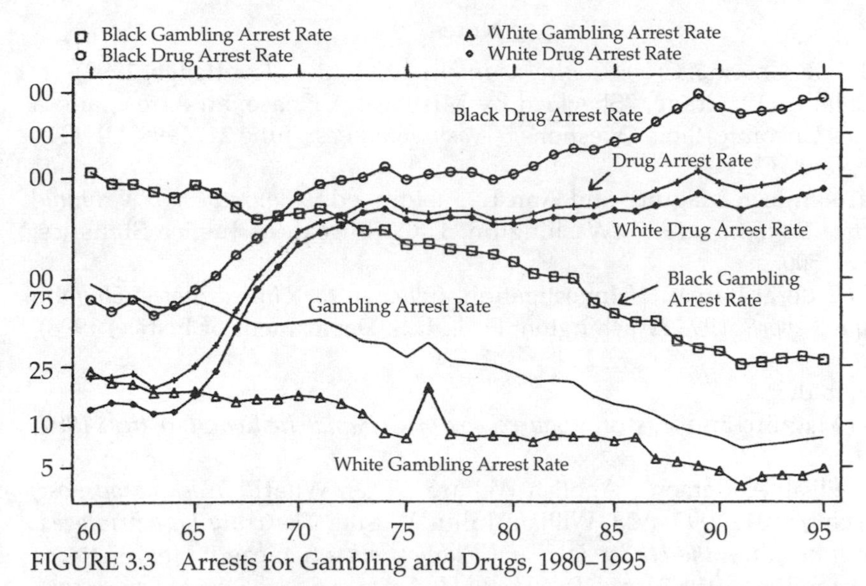

FIGURE 3.3 Arrests for Gambling and Drugs, 1980–1995

SOURCE: Roland J. Chilton, "Drug Prohibition and Other Legislative Folly: Victimless Crime, 1960–1995," (paper delivered to the American Society of Criminology, San Diego, Calif., August 8, 1997).

From the standpoint of law enforcement, with its need to make arrests, the War on Drugs has been a godsend. Prior to 1970, before the War on Drugs became a national obsession, 75 percent of all arrests were for gambling, public indecency, vagrancy, and other petty crimes generally considered "public disorder" offenses. As drug arrests increase, arrests for gambling, prostitution, and vagrancy decline. (See Figure 3.3.) With the War on Drugs, the police no longer need to make arrests for minor offenses to prove that they are doing their job.[11]

The crime control industry has meanwhile become one of the most powerful lobbies in the United States. It is so powerful that the allocation of resources to other institutions, such as welfare and education, has been severely curtailed at the same time that the law enforcement industry, including police, prosecutors, judges, and prisons, has become one of the nation's most important growth industries. Not surprisingly, these policies make the United States the most incarcerating country in the Western world. As we shall see in the next chapter, the so-called War on Drugs is in reality an extension of the war against minorities and the poor.

Notes

1. Nils Christie, *Crime Control as Industry* (London: Routledge, 1993).
2. James O. Crane, "Shackled by Mistrust: A Chase, an Arrest, and a Cop's Uncomfortable Questions," *Washington Post*, June 21, 1998, C1, C4.
3. Ibid., C4.
4. Kathleen Maguire and Ann L. Pastore, eds., *Sourcebook of Criminal Justice Statistics, 1997* (Washington, D.C.: Bureau of Justice Statistics, 1998), 506.
5. Federal Bureau of Investigation, *Crime in the United States: Uniform Crime Reports 1997* (Washington, D.C.: U.S. Department of Justice, 1998), 221.
6. Ibid.
7. Maguire and Pastore, *Sourcebook of Criminal Justice Statistics, 1997*, 240.
8. Elijah Anderson, "Abolish Welfare—Then What?" *Washington Post*, December 31, 1993, A23; William Julius Wilson, *The Truly Disadvantaged: The Inner City, the Underclass, and Public Policy* (Chicago: University of Chicago Press, 1987), and *The Ghetto Underclass: Social Science Perspectives* (New York: Sage Publications, 1993).
9. D. Bayley and H. Mendelsohn, *Minorities and the Police* (New York: Free Press, 1969).
10. I. Wallach and C. Jackson, "Perception of the Police in a Black Community," in J. Snibbe and H. Snibbe, eds., *The Urban Policeman in Transition* (Springfield, Ill.: Charles Thomas, 1973).
11. Roland J. Chilton, "Drug Prohibition and Other Legislative Folly: Victimless Crime, 1960–1995" (paper delivered to the American Society of Criminology, San Diego, Calif., 1997).

Chapter Four

The War on Drugs: America's Ethnic Cleansing

U.S. Surgeon General Jocelyn Elders spoke the unspeakable at a press conference on December 8, 1995. She courageously suggested that the government look at the experience of countries that had decriminalized drugs. She said it was her understanding that in other countries the crime rate and the incidence of drug abuse had actually declined with decriminalization. The White House was apoplectic and dismissed the idea out of hand. The administration's denials came faster than planes flying cocaine from Venezuela to Miami: Under no circumstances would there be such an inquiry.

The administration's response was particularly unfortunate, since the surgeon general did not propose that drugs be legalized, as the U.S. press erroneously reported. She proposed only that we look at the facts to see if the experience of other countries might provide a clue to a better approach than the U.S. War on Drugs, which almost everyone, including Attorney General Janet Reno, acknowledges has been a failure. The ineffectiveness and absurdity of putting so many people in prison for drug offenses has led police chiefs, prison wardens, some big-city mayors, and even some conservative politicians and pundits, including William F. Buckley, former Secretary of State George Schultz, and Nobel economist

Milton Friedman, to speak out in favor of decriminalization. Judges, required by law to sentence drug offenders to long, mandatory sentences, recognize the injustice and folly of the system and often refuse to impose the sentences.[1] On the other hand, drug offenders often are sentenced to terms with no possibility of parole, which means they actually spend more time in prison than most violent offenders.

It is primarily owing to the War on Drugs that U.S. prisons and jails are overflowing. In 1996 there were almost 1 million arrests for drug abuse. Only larceny and driving under the influence accounted for as many arrests as violations of drug laws.[2]

People sentenced to prison for drugs are driving the boom in prison construction and the crime control industry: 60 percent of federal and more than 30 percent of all state prisoners are sentenced for drug offenses.[3] (See Figure 4.1.) Approximately one-third of these are sentenced for marijuana, two-thirds for heroin and cocaine. (Official reports make no distinction between heroin and cocaine, but most of the arrests and prison sentences are for cocaine.)

The people arrested for drugs and receiving lengthy prison sentences are not predatory, habitual criminals. According to a confidential study done at the request of Attorney General Reno, more than 36 percent of all prisoners sentenced for drug offenses are "low level drug offenders with no current or prior violent offenses on their records, no involvement in sophisticated criminal activity and no previous prison time." They are sentenced to an average of almost *seven years* in prison.[4] (See Box 4.1.)

In today's world of overzealous policing of the ghetto, women are being targeted even more than men: Though incarceration rates for drug offenses rose dramatically between 1980 and 1997 for both men and women, the rate of incarceration for female inmates increased at almost twice the rate for males. (See Figure 4.2.)

These data on drug convictions support the conclusions of a study by the National Council on Crime and Delinquency. The study found that more than half of all prisoners in state and federal prisons are being held for offenses that, according to opinion surveys, the general public considers "not very serious crimes."[5]

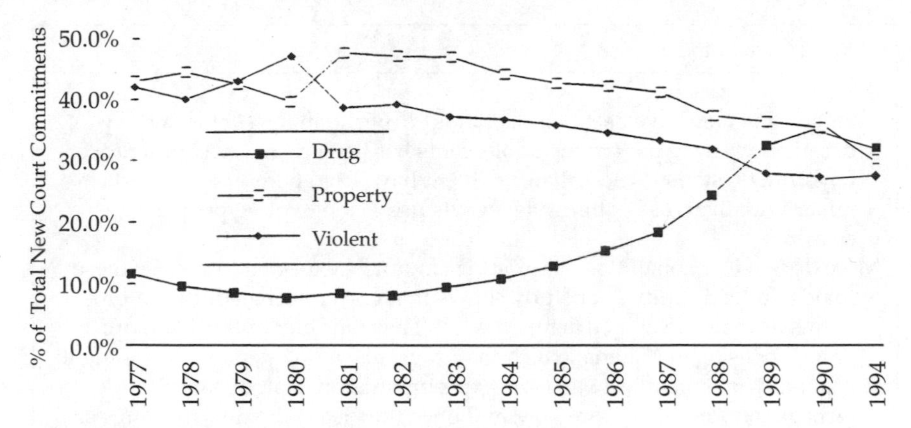

FIGURE 4.1 New Court Commitments to State Prisons by Type of Crime, 1977–1994

SOURCE: Kathleen Maguire and Ann L. Pastore, eds., *Sourcebook of Criminal Justice Statistics* (Washington, D.C.: U.S. Department of Justice, Bureau of Justice Statistics, 1977–1995).

BOX 4.1 Antidrug Programs Miss Mark: Efforts to Curb Heroin Supply Fail to Affect Demand

Marsha Rosenbaum
San Francisco Chronicle, January 8, 1999, A23

There was another heroin overdose in San Francisco last week. This time it was singer Boz Scraggs' 21-year-old son, Oscar. Less than two years ago, Nick Traina, Danielle Steel's 19-year-old son, overdosed on heroin and died. In Plano, Texas, a suburb of Dallas, 11 young people recently died of heroin overdoses.

A natural reaction to these alarming reports is a call for increased efforts to curb availability. The problem is, we're already trying this. The federal drug control budget exceeds $17 billion a year. Add to that state and local budgets for fighting drugs and the figure may be five times larger. Two-thirds of this money is spent to try to stop drugs from entering the country.

So far (perhaps because the black market for drugs generates $64 billion annually), this effort has been a dismal failure. In fact, since President Reagan began escalating the War on Drugs, worldwide production of opium, from which heroin is made, has expanded. The price of heroin has dropped and its purity has increased. We cannot seem to make a dent in the supply, so heroin is still with us.

Our efforts to reduce demand have fared no better than our efforts to reduce supply. Today's young adults were in grade school when Nancy Reagan first began telling them to "just say no." Again and again, in the schools

(continues)

BOX 4.1 *(continued)*

and on TV, they have been warned about drugs' dangers. Yet for nearly a decade now, drug use among adolescents has been rising. According to government statistics, less than 1 percent have tried heroin, but experts familiar with drug-use patterns believe its use among young people is increasing.

More drug education of the sort existing cannot be expected to reverse these trends. Indeed, study after study shows that current drug education programs have no effect on drug use. Why? They lack credibility. Most programs focus on marijuana, which the programs overly demonize, hoping to frighten young people away from experimentation. Half of American teenagers try marijuana anyway, and once they learn the dire warnings are not true, they begin to mistrust everything about drugs that adults tell them. And why shouldn't they? Why should they listen at all if they can't believe what we tell them?

The truth about heroin is that it is much more dangerous than marijuana. Anyone who injects heroin with a used needle risks contracting a deadly infection, such as hepatitis or HIV. Anyone who uses heroin steadily for several weeks will begin to develop physical dependence on it and suffer withdrawal symptoms if they stop.

People who occasionally use heroin do not become addicted. However, compared to the addict, the occasional heroin user who has not developed tolerance to the drug, is at much greater risk for a fatal overdose. Still, because heroin is unregulated and uncontrolled, even the most experienced user cannot know the potency of a batch of unlabeled white powder.

These are the kinds of warnings we should give young people about heroin. But first we have to get them to listen by convincing them they can trust us. They must also trust that they can come to us in an emergency. "Zero tolerance," another method of deterring young people from experimentation, has meant that too many have died because their friends were afraid to call parents or other authorities for help. Terrified of being detected themselves, teenagers in Plano, for example, fled the scene, leaving one boy to choke on his own vomit and die.

Like it or not, we cannot seal our borders or completely eliminate demand for drugs. Moral indignation will not change that reality. A more pragmatic approach would be to learn to live with drugs and to focus on reducing drug-related harm. Our first priority ought to be gaining the trust of young people. We ought to offer a scientifically grounded education that allows them to learn all they can about drugs, alcohol and any other substance(s) they ingest.

Young people will ultimately make their own decisions about drug use. When they do, they ought to have information from sources they trust to ensure their safety.

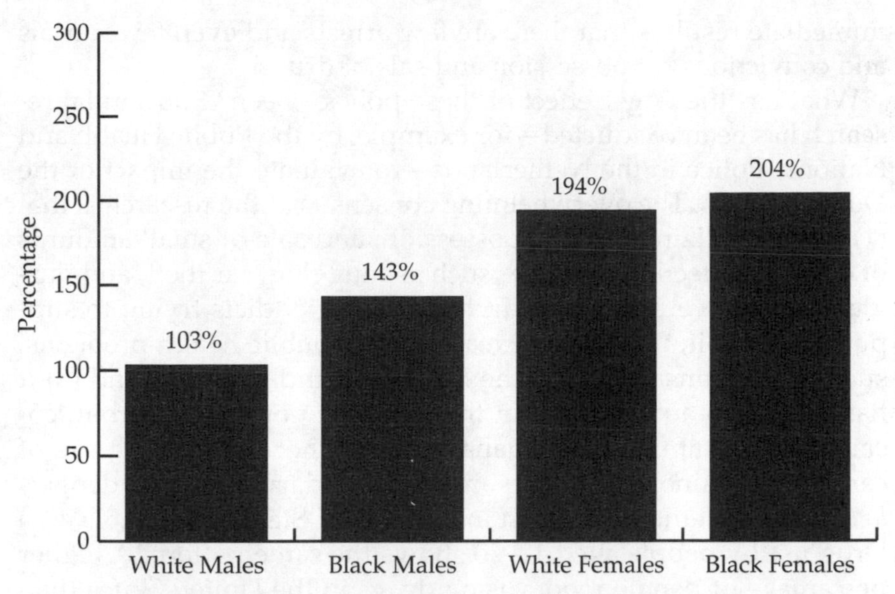

FIGURE 4.2 Percent Change of Sentenced Prisoners in State and Federal Prisons by Sex and Race, 1985–1995

SOURCE: *Bureau of Justice Statistics Bulletin,* June 1997, "Prisoners in 1996," 9.
NOTE: Includes only prisoners sentenced to more than one year.

The Impact of Decriminalization

If Surgeon General Elders's recommendation had been followed and a study of other countries' experiences had been conducted, the findings would at the very least have suggested the United States consider a major shift in policy. The Netherlands, a leader in the search for alternatives to policing as a solution to the social problems associated with the use of drugs,[6] has (1) decriminalized the use and sale of marijuana and (2) de facto decriminalized the possession and sale of small amounts of other drugs. Marijuana and hashish can be purchased in more than 2,000 coffee shops, which even display a drawing of a marijuana plant to advertise the availability of the drug. (Other forms of advertising are prohibited.) Almost every kind of drug is readily available on the streets of major cities in the Netherlands.[7] The underlying premise governing police enforcement of antidrug laws is that the police are to serve as a bridge between drug addicts and treatment services. The immediate result is that there are few arrests and even fewer trials and convictions for possession and sale of drugs.

What has the larger effect of these policies been? Substantial research has been conducted—for example, by the Public Health and National Police in the Netherlands—to evaluate the impact of the Dutch policies. The overwhelming consensus of the research is that (1) decriminalizing the use, possession, and sale of small amounts of drugs has decreased crimes such as mugging, car theft, and burglary, which were formerly driven by drug addicts trying to support their habit; (2) it has decreased other public health problems, such as the transmission of the HIV virus and hepatitis; and (3) it has *not* led to any increase in the frequency of use of heroin, cocaine, amphetamines, marijuana, or any other drugs.[8] The use of cannabis, cocaine, and heroin among secondary school students is *lower* in the Netherlands than in the United States. (See Table 4.1.) Drug use by people aged 12–70 shows the same pattern: A higher percentage of people report using drugs in the United States than in the Netherlands. (See Table 4.2.)

Spain, Switzerland, Denmark, Austria, and Italy have also experimented with alternatives to police-enforced prohibition, and have found similar results. In Denmark, for example, there is a section of the city (Christiana) where hashish and marijuana are openly sold

TABLE 4.1 Drug Use in the United States and the Netherlands, Secondary School Students (ages 13–18)

	13–14 Years		*15–16 Years*		*17–18 Years*	
	United States	*Netherlands*	*United States*	*Netherlands*	*United States*	*Netherlands*
Lifetime						
Cannabis	14.6%	2.6%	35.0%	10.8%	43.7%	17.7%
Cocaine	3.6%	0.6%	7.7%	1.2%	10.3%	1.6%
Heroin	NA[a]	NA	NA	NA	1.3%	0.5%
Past Month						
Cannibis	5.4%	1.3%	14.9%	5.2%	16.7%	4.6%
Cocaine	1.6%	1.2%	2.7%	0.5%	2.8%	0.2%
Heroin	NA	NA	NA	NA	0.3%	0.3%

SOURCE: Michael Elsner, "The Sociology of Reefer Madness: The Criminalization of Marijuana in the USA" (Ph.D. diss., American University, Washington, D.C., 1994).

[a] Not available.

TABLE 4.2 Drug Use in the United States and the Netherlands (ages 12–70)

	Lifetime Use		*Past Year*		*Past Month*	
	Netherlands	*United States*	*Netherlands*	*United States*	*Netherlands*	*United States*
Cannabis	24%	32%	10%	12%	6%	6%
Cocaine	5%	11%	1%	4%	.4%	1%
Heroin	1%	0.8%	.1%	.3%	NA[a]	NA

SOURCE: Michael Elsner, "The Sociology of Reefer Madness: The Criminalization of Marijuana in the USA" (Ph.D. diss., American University, Washington, D.C., 1994).
[a] Not available.

by street vendors. Despite the ready availability of these drugs to people of all ages, there has been no increase in usage among teens or any other age group. Zurich and Geneva have periodically permitted the establishment of "needle parks," that is, places in the city where addicts could go and openly purchase drugs and where the government provided sterile needles and medical help for addicts.[9]

In response to citizen concerns in the cities with open drug markets, the Swiss government closed the open markets and embarked instead on a three-year experiment with "drug vans" that distribute sterile needles in parks where drug users congregate. The head of a medical team that examined the impact of the open drug scene on addicts and the community concluded:

> . . . two major lessons should be learned from the needle park experiment: on the side of the social and medical institutions, the need to work side by side with the communities, the drug users in the street, etc. Secondly, the law and its executive arms, the courts and the police should realize that their influence is limited and potentially harmful but that their role in balancing the interests of drug users and those of the population is essential in helping to create a climate in which drug users can be taken care of not only by in-house specialists but by the whole society.[10]

Spain followed the Netherlands in implementing a de facto decriminalization of drug possession or sale of small amounts. Reports from Spanish police and academics are based on research less carefully conducted than that in the Dutch and Swiss studies, but the results are similar: Neither usage nor crimes associated with

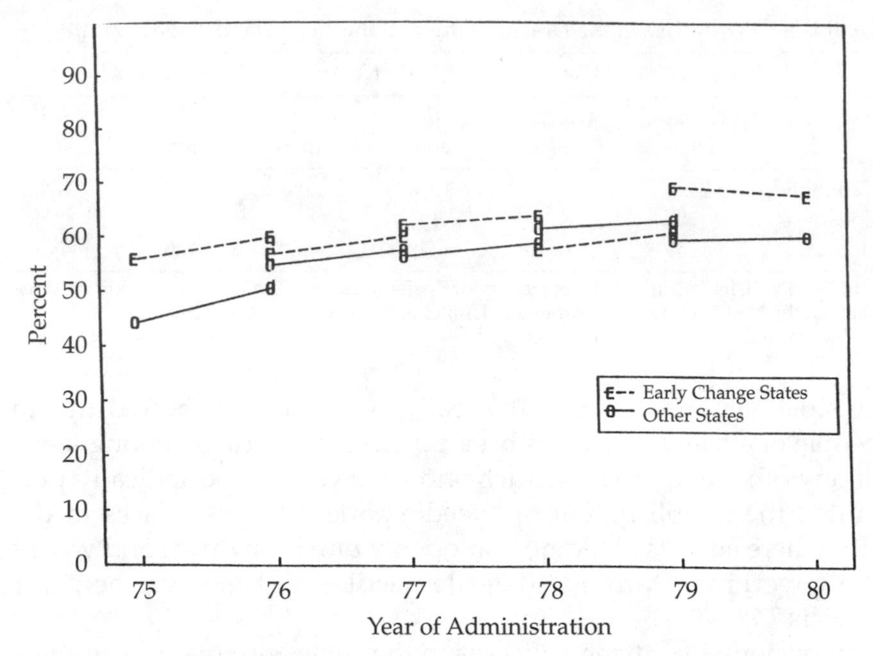

FIGURE 4.3 Lifetime Marijuana Use in States That Have Versus States That Have Not Decriminalized Marijuana (12th-Grade Students)

SOURCE: Lloyd D. Johnston, Patrick M. O'Malley, and Jerald G. Bachman, *Marijuana Decriminalization: The Impact on Youth, 1975–1980* (Ann Arbor: Institute for Social Research, University of Michigan, 1981), 31.

drug dealing rose appreciably, and diseases associated with drug use declined.

Ironically, the surgeon general did not need to go to the Netherlands for data on the impact of decriminalization: Eleven U.S. states (Alaska, California, Colorado, Maine, Minnesota, Mississippi, New York, North Carolina, Ohio, Oregon, and Utah) have at one time or another decriminalized the possession of small amounts of marijuana. Surveys of high school and college students' use of marijuana from 1975 to 1980 (after decriminalization) shows no difference in the frequency of use among students in states that have decriminalized marijuana and those in states that have not. (See Figure 4.3.) Comparison of prevalence of use shows "convincing evidence that there is no systematic gain or loss" in marijuana usage.[11]

There is other evidence that de facto decriminalization reduces crimes associated with drugs, especially murder and violence. In Seattle, Washington, where I conducted a ten-year study of organized crime, I found that when the police were taking bribes and protecting drug dealers, murders and assaults associated with drug dealing were low, but when the police enforced antidrug laws these offenses increased appreciably.[12] The reason is quite simple: When the police cooperate with drug dealers they essentially give them an informal "license" to traffic in certain areas of the city. Competitors are "discouraged" by being arrested. Since they face no competition, the "licensed" dealers do not need to resort to violence to protect their territory; they need only call their partners on the police force and have their competitors arrested.

Decriminalization has positive effects that go well beyond a reduction in the violence and crime associated with drug dealing. The risk of getting AIDS, hepatitis, and other diseases through shared needles and the human suffering and deaths caused by impure drugs are well known to users, but they are ineffective deterrents. Otherwise, the rates of drug use would have declined with the onset of AIDS and the knowledge that the risks of intravenous injection had gone up.

The Consequences

The War on Drugs in the United States has produced another war as well: It is a war between the police and minority youth from the ghetto. One need only listen to the words of "gangsta rap" music to get a sense of the hostility, the war mentality that permeates the ghetto. Young black and Latino men living in America's ghettos and barrios are under siege from and at war with the police. Riots erupted in Los Angeles when the white police officers who beat Rodney King were slapped on the wrist. And whereas the white population thought O. J. Simpson's guilt had been proved "beyond a reasonable doubt," the black population believed he was not guilty. The chasm between black and white in the United States grows deeper by the day, and the police, prosecutors, courts, and prisons are the steam shovel digging it wider.

TABLE 4.3 Drug Arrests, State Court Convictions, and Drug Use by Race and Ethnicity (percent)

	Drug Use					
	Marijuana	*Heroin*	*LSD*	*Cocaine*	*Crack*	*Any Illegal*
White	14.2	1.2	9.1	0.8	0.3	18.3
Black	10.5	1.4	2.1	1.0	0.6	14.3
Hispanic	12.3	0.9	4.9	1.1	0.3	15.5

	Arrests and Convictions		
	Arrested	*Convicted of Possession*	*Convicted of Trafficking*
White	60.4%	46%	37%
Black	38.4%	53%	63%
Hispanic	NA[a]	NA	NA

SOURCES: Lloyd D. Johnston, Patrick M. O'Malley, and Jerald G. Bachman, "National Survey Results on Drug Use from Monitoring the Future, 1995–1997," *National Institute on Drug Abuse (NIDA)* (Washington, D.C.: U.S. Department of Health and Human Services, 1998), 74–77; Federal Bureau of Investigation, *Crime in the United States Uniform Crime Reports* (Washington, D.C.: U.S. Department of Justice, 1997), 235; Kathleen Maguire and Ann L. Pastore, eds., *Sourcebook of Criminal Justice Statistics, 1997* (Washington, D.C.: U.S. Department of Justice, Bureau of Justice Statistics, 1998), 247–249, 422.

[a] Not available.

Young black men make up about 6 percent of the population but 40 percent of those arrested for drug possession and trafficking and more than 50 percent of those convicted of violating drug laws. (See Table 4.3.) The white male population, which is five times as large as the black male population, accounts for only 37 percent of those convicted of drug offenses, despite the fact that, as national household surveys show, whites are more likely to use illegal drugs than either blacks or Latinos. White high school students are more frequent users of illegal drugs of all kinds than are black students.[13] (See Table 3.2.)

African American women and juveniles are particularly hard hit by the racially inequitable enforcement of drug laws. The number of women in state and federal prisons increased fourfold in the last twenty years of the twentieth century. The majority of female inmates are in prison for drugs, and the impact of this on black families is staggering, since 75 percent of the black female inmates are mothers. Discrimination in sentencing for black juveniles is incomprehensible by any standard. The number of white juveniles in locked detention for drugs has *declined* since 1985, whereas the number of nonwhite juveniles (mostly black) in locked detention has increased by 259 percent.

It is revealing to compare the different enforcement patterns for laws prohibiting driving under the influence (DUI) and antidrug laws. DUI is the second most frequently committed crime in the United States. It is objectively one of the most harmful crimes: Property costs from accidents resulting from drunk driving are astronomical. It is estimated that 40 percent of automobile accident deaths are the result of drunken driving.[14] Drunk driving is committed primarily by whites: Nearly 90 percent of those arrested for DUI are white. But DUI offenders are rarely sentenced to prison, and disproportionately many of those who are, are black. Cathy Shine and Marc Mauer conclude from their study of New York and California that

> Data . . . show that the typical sentence for a drunk driver is either some combination of fines, probation, and treatment or a brief jail sentence. Fewer than 1 percent of convicted drunk drivers in these states receive a prison term . . . overall, African-Americans and Hispanics receive harsher penalties than whites for this offense.[15]

Yet DUI may be the single most dangerous of those crimes committed frequently:

> In the stereotype world, violence is largely the product of "guns-and-drugs" and gangs. That's a dangerous falsehood. The United States has had the industrial world's highest homicide rates for some 150 years. The 1986 homicide rate for young white males in the United States was twice as high as the rate for all young men in other industrialized nations. In reality, the heavily advertised legal drug alcohol is the drug most likely to lead to violence and death. Alcohol is associated with more homicides nationally than illicit drugs, and almost the same number of people are killed annually by drunk drivers as are murdered; drunk drivers are overwhelmingly white males.[16]

The Corruption of Due Process

The Loss of Civil Liberties

The panic over crime has led to undermining the protections against unchecked police powers guaranteed by the U.S. Constitution. Nowhere is this more apparent than in the expansion of the

BOX 4.2 The Snitch

On Tuesday, January 12, 1999, PBS aired a program on the use of informants. A summary of some of the salient findings of the program follows.

In the last five years, nearly a third of defendants in federal drug trafficking cases had their sentences reduced because they informed on other people. Some informants did not serve any time at all. In recent years informants have become key players in the criminal justice system. One prosecuting attorney interviewed frankly admitted that without promising suspects a lesser sentence or probation in return for their testimony implicating other people, it would be virtually impossible to get convictions. The issue raised by these practices, however, is whether the testimony of people promised lighter sentences or no jail time at all can be depended upon.

Several cases of the questionable consequences of using informants illustrate the problems. Clarence Aaron, a college student on an athletic scholarship, drove some friends from one town to another. He was paid $1,500 to introduce them to some people in another town who dealt drugs. When his friends, including his cousin, were caught, they were offered a deal: Their sentence would be reduced if they would inform on Clarence. They agreed. All four of the witnesses testifying against Clarence had previous criminal records. Clarence had none. One of the informants, who admitted being a drug kingpin, was sentenced to twelve years in prison, two served less than five years, and Clarence's cousin was given probation. Clarence was sentenced to three life terms without parole. Clarence's defense attorney, Dennis Knizeley, says: "What makes this the worst case I ever had was there was absolutely no cocaine introduced into evidence, there was no cocaine seen . . . the police had no cocaine, the FBI had no cocaine . . . no fingerprints, nothing, the entirety of the case was based upon the testimony of what they call 'cooperating individuals.'"

Cases like Clarence's are legally possible because of the conspiracy laws, which make it a crime to conspire to sell, distribute, or obtain drugs even if there is never any direct involvement in purchasing or selling them.

In another case, the son of Ms. Lulu May Smith of Mobile, Alabama, was identified as a crack dealer. When he learned of the indictment he fled. Ms. Smith was arrested and charged with conspiracy to distribute cocaine, although there was no evidence she had anything to do with her son's dealing; he merely lived in her house. The prosecutor openly admitted that he was using Ms. Smith as bait to force her son to return. When he did not return, Ms. Smith was prosecuted and sentenced to seven years in prison.

police right to stop and frisk ordinary citizens. The leading decision was handed down in *Terry v. Ohio* (1968), which gave police the right to stop and frisk anyone on the basis of "reasonable suspicion." The power of police over ordinary citizens was further expanded in January 2000, when the U.S. Supreme Court ruled that police officers can pursue and stop people who run from police even if officers have no reason to suspect them of violating the law. In a Chicago case, Sam Wardlow saw a police car turn a corner and began running in the opposite direction. The court held that the police had the right to pursue him and that "a person's nervous, evasive behavior" as well as "headlong flight" are sufficient to give an officer justification for pursuing a suspect.

The fourth Amendment of the U.S. Constitution guarantees the following:

> The right of the people to be secure in their persons, houses, papers, and effects, against unreasonable searches and seizures, shall not be violated, and no Warrants shall issue, but upon probable cause, supported by Oath or affirmation, and particularly describing the place to be searched, and the persons or things to be seized.

As Timothy Lynch points out, "The key difference between a free society and a totalitarian regime is the power of police agents. In a free society the police are governed by law, whereas in a totalitarian regime the police are the law."[17] Residents living in black and Latino lower-class neighborhoods experience the police as the law and live in a virtual totalitarian state.

All too often, officers policing urban ghettoes believe there is "reasonable suspicion" to stop and search any young black or Latino man they see on the streets or, in the case of Amadou Diallo, standing in a doorway.

In February 1999 Diallo was shot nineteen times in a hail of forty-one bullets fired by four plainclothes New York City police officers. The officers were members of a special so-called elite Street Crimes Unit. One of the officers claimed that he thought Diallo looked like a suspected serial rapist who had been terrorizing the neighborhood. The four officers dressed in jeans and sweatshirts exited from their unmarked car, drew their weapons, and told Diallo to stop. Diallo, the officers said, moved his hand toward his waist. One of the officers hollered "gun!" and the police opened fire. Diallo died on the stoop of his own apartment building. He was a street vendor without a criminal record, not the suspected serial rapist. The police officers were tried and found not guilty of second-degree murder, depraved indifference to human life, and reckless endangerment.

New York City Mayor Rudy Giuliani has been among the most outspoken advocates of getting tough on crime. A former prosecutor, Giuliani encouraged the police to use extreme measures in an effort to clean up the streets. Giuliani's police commissioner, William Bratton, created the special Street Crimes Unit, staffed by eighty-six policemen (rapidly increased to 380) who patrolled the poorest sections of the city in unmarked cars and dressed in jeans and sweatshirts, as described by Lynch:

> The members were known as the "commandos" of the NYPD and they often spoke of "retaking neighborhoods" from the criminal element. In 1996 some of the officers distributed T-shirts emblazoned with the following quotation from Ernest Hemingway: "Certainly there is no hunting like the hunting of man, and those who have hunted armed men long enough and liked it, never really care for anything else thereafter."[18]

Naturally, under the rules of bureaucratic organization the Street Crimes Unit was accountable not to the residents of the ghettos where they patrolled nightly but to the higher-ups in the police department. Their work was measured in terms of their "productivity," which was measured by the number of gun and drug seizures they made: "Sometimes they stopped thugs and found guns or drugs. More often than not, they stopped innocent people and found empty pockets. The modus operandi of the unit was to quickly swarm on a person with pistols drawn, all the while barking commands laced with vulgarities."[19] In 1998 prosecutors threw out 18,000 arrests for lack of evidence. Judges threw out over half of the 200 felony gun cases brought by the Street Crimes Unit in 1997–1998.

The root causes of the Diallo killing runs deeper, however, than simply the overzealous policing of a bunch of police commandos. The root causes were threefold: the expansion of police powers granted by the Supreme Court in Terry, the political ambitions of Mayor Giuliani and his police commissioners, and the organization of policing that judged performance by arrests and the seizure of guns and drugs.

The Corruption of Due Process

One of the more pernicious side effects of the War on Drugs is the growing use of informants who are promised protection from or leniency in sentencing in return for testimony implicating others.

This practice has accurately been portrayed as little more than government bribery of witnesses. It raises serious questions about the reliability of witnesses' testimony, since witnesses willing to testify against others are rewarded with reduced sentences and sometimes cash payments. (See Box 4.2.)

The case of Javier Cruz is typical. Cruz, allegedly a major drug trafficker in Miami, was accused of murdering Mark Garrett. To avoid conviction on the murder charge, Cruz agreed to work as an informant for the Drug Enforcement Agency (DEA). Cruz testified against other drug dealers, who on the basis of his testimony were sentenced to long prison sentences. For his cooperation Cruz was allowed to plead guilty to manslaughter instead of first-degree murder and was sentenced to only 16 *months* in prison. In addition, all of the drug trafficking charges against Cruz—which carried a mandatory life imprisonment sentence—were dropped.

The question raised by cases like this one is not just whether "justice" in some abstract sense is accomplished. The more telling issue is whether the information and testimony of someone paid off with a short prison sentence—someone who is otherwise facing life behind bars—should be relied upon to put other people in prison.

The trial and conviction of Manuel Antonio Noriega (Panama's former president and a former CIA operative) is a case in point. To obtain Noriega's conviction, federal prosecutors relied almost entirely on the testimony of convicted drug dealers, whom they bribed to testify against Noriega.[20] The bribes the government paid included hundreds of thousands of dollars in cash as well as reduced prison sentences and promises of a lifetime of support and protection under the witness protection program.[21] Those who testified against Noriega included:

Carlos Lehder: A major figure in an international drug trafficking cartel who in 1988 had been sentenced to life plus 135 years in prison for drug trafficking, Lehder was released from prison and with his family given a lifetime income and put into the witness protection program.

Luis del Cid: Charges against del Cid could have sent him to prison for seventy years. In return for his testimony against Noriega, prosecutors recommended a ten-year maximum sentence (he will be eligible for parole after three and a half years), the dropping of deportation procedures, and the release of $94,000 in his pension account, which the government had confiscated.

Max Mermelstein: Accused of organizing transportation of drugs through Panama, Mermelstein was facing a prison sentence of life plus ninety years. For his testimony he was released after two years and twenty-one days, paid $700,000, put into the witness protection program, and promised yearly payments for living expenses.

Floyd Carlton: Carlton, a pilot, was charged with smuggling 880 pounds of cocaine into the United States. His testimony was rewarded with a nine-year suspended prison sentence and three years' probation.

Bribing witnesses to testify in court makes a mockery of criminal justice. Prosecuting attorneys are judged effective if they have a high rate of convictions, which encourages them to overlook questionable testimony from witnesses with something to gain from lying. Relying on informants also leads to the government providing protection for people whose crimes are often more serious than the crimes committed by those the informant testifies against.

The combination of pressure to make arrests and the fact that drug enforcement agents often think they "know who is a dealer" leads agents to plant drugs on suspects. For example, Robert Sobel, of the Los Angeles County Sheriff's Department narcotics unit, testified in March 1993 that seven narcotics agents had planted cocaine in the bag of a suspected dealer. In Oakland, California, drug agents were found guilty of planting drugs and of beating and sexually assaulting suspects. A Los Angeles County Sheriff's Department officer planted heroin on a woman to whom he owed money. These are but a smattering of cases. We do not know how common the practice is of illegally planting drugs on suspects or in their homes, but that it happens at all reflects structural problems in law enforcement that we cannot afford to ignore.

Finally, legislation in the 1990s has dramatically increased the incentive for law enforcement officials to plant evidence and to gain convictions through distortions, lies, and the bribing of witnesses. Houses, cars, boats, airplanes, and other personal property can be seized and sold if the owner is arrested for possessing drugs. The agency making the arrest keeps a percentage of the value, ordinarily 50 or 60 percent. The abuse of these laws is rampant. In Louisiana, according to a report on *Dateline,* police officers began seizing the property of motorists who were stopped and arrested even when there was no evidence of drugs in their possession.

International Consequences

As dire as the consequences of the War on Drugs are for the United States and its citizens, the impact on foreign countries may be even more devastating. The international market in opium, heroin, cocaine, and marijuana is estimated at between $200 and $400 billion a year—a sum larger than the gross national product of all but the ten wealthiest nations in the world and all but a handful of multinational corporations. As a consequence, whole nation-states—Bolivia, Colombia, Laos, Malaysia, Mexico, Pakistan, Peru, Puerto Rico, Thailand, and Turkey—depend upon opium, coca, and hemp production for their agricultural base, and the manufacture of heroin, cocaine, and marijuana is a significant productive sector of the economy.[22] The export of cocaine provides Bolivia with more income than all other export products combined.[23] The production and distribution of illegal drugs are so deeply enmeshed in other nations, including the United States, that their economies would be severely damaged were the international market in drugs to dry up. It is estimated, for example, that marijuana is the second largest cash crop in the United States.

International money laundering of drug profits is the mainstay of countries across the globe, from small island nations in the Caribbean to Mexico, Nigeria, and Switzerland. If the profits were taken out of the international drug market, the economic impact would create a global disaster.

Conclusion

Clinton's response to the surgeon general's proposal was consistent with the irrational response of government officials since the

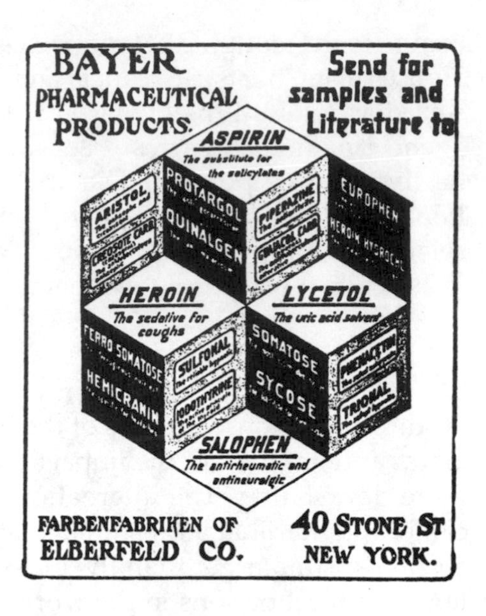

FIGURE 4.4 Bayer Pharmaceuticals Advertisement

In the 1900s the Bayer Pharmaceutical Company developed the drug heroin as a substitute for opium. At the time, the company claimed that heroin was less addictive but had marvelous curative powers. Advertisements such as this one were placed in leading magazines across the United States to attract consumers. During this time opium and cocaine frequently were added to medicines.

1940s. William Bradford Reynolds, assistant attorney general under George Bush, expressed the same irrational, knee-jerk response in a memo to the "heads of department components" in the Department of Justice: "Overall, we should send the message that there are two ways to approach drugs: the soft, easy way that emphasizes drug treatment and rehabilitation versus the hard, tough approach that emphasizes strong law enforcement measures and drug testing. Naturally, we favor the latter." Why should the Justice Department "naturally favor" strong law enforcement measures and drug testing over treatment and rehabilitation? Because they think it will work better? Because there is evidence of its beneficial consequences? Hardly. Favoring the "hard, tough approach" is an ideology; it is part of the law enforcement definition of reality. It is the same kind of ignorant response to social problems that led to burning witches and public executions.

Since drug use was criminalized in the United States (between 1914 and 1937) there has been a steady and constant increase in the availability of drugs and in the number of drug users. Marijuana and cocaine are readily available on every college campus and in every office building, not to mention the streets of every city. Since 1975 the Institute for Social Research at the University of Michigan has been conducting anonymous surveys of high school and college students' use of illegal drugs. Every year more than half the students surveyed admit to using an illegal drug. About 35 percent admit to ever having used illegal drugs.[24] A quarter of a million respondents admit to using it weekly.

Despite spending billions of dollars to fight the War on Drugs and imprisoning hundreds of thousands of young adults, drugs are of higher quality, cheaper, and more readily available than ever. The argument that decriminalizing drugs would increase their availability ignores the fact that criminalizing them has in no way decreased their availability.[25] But furthermore, the data from countries that have decriminalized drugs suggest that decriminalization accompanied by restricted access and *honest* warnings of their potential hazards *would* lead to a reduction in usage.

Most people who use cocaine and marijuana are occasional users. Most users have no trouble stopping if they decide to. Only 3 percent of the people who tried cocaine reported problems giving it up. The number of people who use marijuana is much higher, but the proportion of those who report difficulty giving it up, even after a long period of heavy usage, is negligible. The most highly addictive of these illegal drugs are the opiates and their derivatives (particularly heroin). We do not have good data on the addiction rate among opium users, but we do know that when opium was legally and easily available to addicts through medical doctors, as it was in Great Britain until the 1970s, the illegal drug market and the number of new addicts was minuscule compared to that in the United States.

It is informative to compare the addictive qualities of illegal drugs with those of tobacco and alcohol. A survey asked high school seniors who admitted to using marijuana, cocaine, or cigarettes if they had ever had difficulty stopping. Less than 4 percent reported difficulty stopping cocaine use, compared to 7 percent for marijuana and 18 percent for cigarettes.[26]

We know very well what will work to reduce drug consumption: cigarette smoking and alcohol consumption have been significantly affected by education programs; alcohol and nicotine addicts benefit substantially from self-help groups. Community groups, such as Alcoholics Anonymous, are effective for dealing with that small percentage of people who become addicted. If the currently banned drugs were legal and if their use did not carry the stigma of criminality, problem drug users would seek the help they need. Addicts would not have to pay outlandishly high prices for drugs ($4,000 worth of cocaine in Colombia sells for $20,000 wholesale in Miami, $70,000 on the streets), share dirty needles, or risk illness and even death from impure drugs. Decriminalization would also facilitate the accurate dissemination of knowledge about the drugs. Everyone knows the difference between the effects of beer, wine, and whiskey. Possessing this knowledge enables all of us to choose rationally which to drink under what circumstances. The law enforcement propaganda that lumps all illegal drugs together as equally dangerous makes sensible policies and rational personal decisions impossible. It reinforces the belief on the part of potential users that everything they hear about drugs is a big lie. Every twelve year old in the ghetto knows that marijuana is very different from cocaine, but they are not told exactly how and why. When they are choosing between cocaine, crack, and heroin, they do not have the necessary information even to consider what the difference might be. All they know is that their experiences contradict what they see as the lies and propaganda of the government.

If the Clinton administration had looked objectively at the facts, as the surgeon general suggested, it would not have found a utopian solution in the policies of other countries. No one in the Netherlands, Switzerland, Spain, or the twelve states that have decriminalized marijuana believes that they have found the perfect solution to problems associated with drugs. The fact is that an ideal solution does not exist. Drugs have been part of people's lives in every culture forever. What is needed is an exploration of the best way to deal with the reality, not a blind adherence to failed policies.

The surgeon general's call for a study to see if alternative policies might be more effective was a breath of fresh air. The Clinton administration's response was a throwback to the knee-jerk conservative moralism that created the disaster that is our current policies, with all its attendant human tragedies. Sadly, shortly after Jocelyn Elders made her courageous statement, her son was arrested for selling cocaine. One might have hoped that the arrest of the son of one of his cabinet members would cause the president to reconsider his position, especially in light of the facts that his own brother served time in prison for marijuana use, that he himself admitted smoking marijuana (even though he says he did not inhale), and that one of his classmates at Oxford observed that Clinton was allergic to all kinds of smoke but was quite happy to take his hashish in brownies.

But none of these experiences has swayed Clinton's unswerving support for the failed U.S. drug policies, policies which could have sent him to prison and which are stupid and inhumane. Instead, he has strengthened his commitment to the pursuit of a winless war. Meanwhile, under the guise of fighting drugs, the war on the poor and minorities grows ever more ferocious.

Notes

1. T. Thompson, "Mandatory Terms: Routinely Evaded but Still Popular," *Washington Post*, September 24, 1991, A21.

2. Federal Bureau of Investigation, *Crime in the United States, 1997: Uniform Crime Reports* (Washington, D.C.: U.S. Department of Justice, 1998), 217.

3. Kathleen Maguire, and Ann Pastore, *Sourcebook of Criminal Justice Statistics, 1997* (Washington, D.C.: Bureau of Justice Statistics, 1998), 506, 623, 636.

4. "An Analysis of Non-Violent Drug Offenders with Minimal Criminal Histories," U.S. Department of Justice, Washington, D.C., February 1994, 2–3.

5. J. Austin and J. Irwin. *Who Goes to Prison*? (San Francisco: National Council on Crime and Delinquency, 1987).

6. M. Grapendaal, E. Leuw, and H. Nelen, "Drugs and Crime in an Accommodating Social Context: The Situation in Amsterdam," *Contemporary Drug Problems* 19 (Summer 1992): 303–326; G. Wijngaart, "The Dutch Approach: Normalization of Drug Problems," *Journal of Drug Issues* 20 (Fall 1990): 667–678; H. Vliet, "Separation of Drug Markets and the Normalization of Drug Problems in the Netherlands: An Example for Other Countries?" *Journal of Drug Issues* 20 (Summer 1990): 463–471.

7. Vliet, "Separation of Drug Markets."

8. MacCoun, Peter Reuter, and Thomas Schelling, "Assessing Alternative Drug Control Regimes," *Journal of Policy Analysis and Management* 15, no. 3 (1996): 330–352.

9. Manuel Eisner, "Policies Towards Open Drug Scenes and Street Crime: The Case of the City of Zurich," *European Journal on Criminal Policy and Research* 1, no. 2 (1994): 61–75.

10. Peter J. Grob, "The Needle Park in Zurich: The Story and the Lessons To Be Learned," *European Journal on Criminal Policy and Research* 1, no. 2 (1994): 59–60.

11. Lloyd D. Johnston, Patrick O'Malley, and Jerold G. Bachman, "Marijuana Decriminalization: The Impact on Youth, 1975–1980. Monitoring the Future Occasional Paper 13" (Institute for Social Research, University of Michigan, Ann Arbor, 1981), 18.

12. William J. Chambliss, *On the Take: From Petty Crooks to Presidents*, rev. ed. (Bloomington: Indiana University Press, 1988).

13. Lloyd D. Johnston, Patrick O'Malley, and Jerold G. Bachman, "Monitoring the Future Occasional Paper 19" (Institute for Social Research, University of Michigan, Ann Arbor, 1991); National Institute of Drug Abuse, *National Household Survey on Drug Abuse: Population Estimates, 1991* (Washington, D.C.: NIDA, 1991), 19–21.

14. National Highway Traffic Safety Administration (1998).

15. Cathy Shine and Marc Mauer, *Does the Punishment Fit the Crime? Drug Users and Drunk Drivers: Questions of Race and Class* (Washington, D.C.: The Sentencing Project, 1993).

16. Peter Medoff and Holly Sklar, *Streets of Hope: The Fall and Rise of an Urban Neighborhood* (Boston: South End Press, 1994), 210–211.

17. Timothy Lynch, "We Own the Night: Amadou Diallo's Deadly Encounter with New York City's Street Crimes Unit" (Washington, D.C.: Cato Institute, March 31, 2000), 4.

18. Ibid., 4.

19. Ibid.

20. "Noriega: How the Feds Got Their Man," Newsweek, April 20, 1992, 37; G. Gugliotta, "The Sleaze Connection," Washington Post, September 22, 1991, C1.

21. "Noriega: How the Feds Got Their Man," 23.

22. A. Salamat, "Opiate of the Frontier: Pakistani Tribes Find It Hard To Give Up Poppy Crop," *Far Eastern Economic Review* 156 (May 27, 1993): 18; "The General and the Cocaleros," *The Economist* 313 (December 9, 1989): 40–41; "Fighting Drugs," *The Economist* 328 (August 7, 1987): 39–40; M. Colett, "Cocaine Capitalism," *New Statesman and Society* 1 (August 12, 1988): 14–17; "The Cocaine Economies: Latin America's Killing Fields," *The Economist* 309 (October 8, 1988): 21ff.; J. Grimond, "The Other Obstacles to Change," *The Economist* 329 (November 13, 1993): 25–27; "Under the Influence," *The Economist* 312 (September 30, 1989): 38ff.; B. Lintner, "Poisons and Politics," *Far Eastern Economic Review* 154 (November 14, 1991): 52–54; "Sex, Drugs, and Radicals," *The Economist* 311 (April 8, 1989): 54ff.

23. "The Cocaine Economies."

24. U.S. Department of Health and Human Services, *National Household Survey on Drug Abuse: Population Estimates, 1996* (Washington, D.C.: Substance Abuse and Mental Health Service Administration, 1997), 17.
25. Lloyd D. Johnston, Patrick O'Malley, and Jerold G. Bachman, *Monitoring the Future* (Institute for Social Research, University of Michigan, Ann Arbor, January 25, 1992).
26. Lloyd D. Johnston, Patrick O'Malley, and Jerold G. Bachman, "Monitoring the Future Occasional Paper 9" (Institute for Social Research, University of Michigan, Ann Arbor, 1981), 1.

Chapter Five

Finding Crime II: The White Lower Class

The police, prosecutors, and courts have an insatiable need for offenders in order to justify their existence, and poor minorities bear the brunt of that need. But poor minorities are not the only ones who suffer being processed and labeled deviant. Working-class youths in the suburbs and small towns are the "functional equivalent" of the ghetto poor. In these communities the police and prosecutors turn the same blind eye on the delinquencies of middle- and upper-class youths they do on those of college and university students in the cities. But here it is the working- and lower-class youths who attract the attention and suffer the consequences reserved for the minorities in the urban areas. The underlying cause of the selective enforcement of the law is the same: The bureaucratic requirement that police action be designed to maximize rewards and minimize strain for the organization leads to looking for crime among the powerless and ignoring the crimes of the powerful—including the children of the powerful.

How the police, the schools, and other community organizations effect this is illustrated by a comparison of the delinquencies and police encounters of two gangs of high school boys whom I observed over a two-year period. I call these gangs the "Saints" and the "Roughnecks," not because of their behavior but because of how their behavior was perceived by key people in their community.

The Saints were a group of eight promising young men from "good" white, upper-middle-class families. They attended Hanibal High: a moderate size high school in a suburb near a large metropolitan area.[1] The Saints were active in school affairs, were enrolled in the precollege program, and received good grades. At the same time, they were some of the most delinquent boys at Hanibal High.

The teachers, their parents, and people in the community knew that these boys occasionally sowed a few wild oats. They were totally unaware, however, of the extent of the Saints' delinquency. No one realized that "sowing their wild oats" completely occupied the daily routine of these young men. The Saints were constantly occupied in truancy, drinking, wild driving, petty theft, and vandalism. Yet not one was officially arrested for any misdeed during the two years I observed them.

This record was particularly surprising in light of my observations during the same two years of another gang of Hanibal High students, the six lower-class white boys I call the Roughnecks. The Roughnecks were constantly in trouble with the police and the community, even though their rate of delinquency was about the same as that of the Saints. What caused this disparity? What was its result? The following consideration of the activities, social class, and community perceptions of both gangs may provide some answers.

The Saints

The Saints from Monday to Friday

The Saints' principal daily concern was to get out of school as early as possible. They managed, with minimum danger of being accused of playing hooky, through an elaborate procedure for obtaining "legitimate" release from class. The most common technique was for one boy to obtain the release of another by fabricating a meeting of some committee, program, or recognized club. Charles might raise his hand in his 9:00 chemistry class and ask to be excused—a euphemism for going to the bathroom. Charles would go to Ed's math class and inform the teacher that Ed was needed for a 9:30 rehearsal of the drama club play. The math teacher would recognize Ed and Charles as "good students" involved in numerous school activities and would permit Ed to leave at 9:30. Charles would return to his class, and Ed would go to Tom's English class to obtain his release. Tom would engineer Charles's escape. The strategy would continue until as many of the Saints as possible were freed. After a stealthy trip to the car (which had been parked in a strategic spot), the boys were off for a day of fun.

Over the two years that I observed and interviewed the Saints, this pattern was repeated nearly every day. There were variations on the theme, but in one form or another the boys used this procedure to get out of class and then off the school grounds. Rarely did all eight of the Saints manage to leave school at the same time—the average number avoiding school on the days I observed them was five.

Having escaped from the concrete corridors the boys usually went either to a pool hall on the other (lower-class) side of town or to a café in the suburbs. Both places were out of the way of people the boys were likely to know (family or school officials), and both provided a source of entertainment. The pool hall's entertainment was the generally rough atmosphere, the occasional hustler, the sometimes drunk proprietor, and, of course, the game of pool. The café's entertainment was provided by harassing the owner. The boys would "accidentally" knock a glass on the floor or spill cola on the counter—not all the time, but enough to be sporting. They would also bend spoons, put salt in sugar bowls, and generally tease whoever was working in the café. Since the boys' business was substantial (between the horsing around and the teasing they did buy food and drinks), the owner tolerated their transgressions.

The Saints on Weekends

On weekends the automobile was even more critical to the Saints' activities than it was during the week, for on weekends the Saints went to Big Town—a large city with a population of more than a million, twenty-five miles from Hanibal. Every Friday and Saturday night most of the Saints would meet between 8:00 and 8:30 to go into Big Town, where they drank heavily in taverns or nightclubs, drove drunkenly through the streets, committed acts of vandalism, and played pranks.

By midnight on Fridays and Saturdays the Saints were usually thoroughly high, and one or two of them were often so drunk they had to be carried to the cars. Then they drove around town, calling obscenities to women and girls, occasionally trying (unsuccessfully so far as I could tell) to pick up girls, and driving recklessly through red lights and at high speeds with their lights out. Occasionally they played chicken. In another game, one boy would climb out the back window of their car and across the roof to the driver's side while the car was moving at high speed (between forty and fifty miles an hour); then the driver would move over and the boy who had just crawled across the roof would take the driver's seat.

Searching for "fair game" for a prank was the boys' principal activity after leaving a tavern. They would drive alongside a foot patrolman and ask directions to some street. If the policeman leaned on the car in the course of answering the question, the driver would speed away, causing him to lose his balance. The Saints were careful to play this prank only in an area where they were not going to spend much time and where they could quickly disappear around a corner to avoid having their license plate number taken.

Construction sites and road repair areas were the special province of the Saints' mischief. A soon-to-be-repaired hole in the road inevitably invited them to remove the lanterns and wooden barricades and put them in the car, leaving the hole unprotected. They would find a safe vantage point and wait for an unsuspecting motorist to drive into the hole. Often, though not always, the boys would go up to the motorist and commiserate with him about the dreadful way the city protected its citizenry.

Leaving the scene of the open hole and the motorist, the boys would then go searching for an appropriate place to erect the stolen barricades. An "appropriate place" was often a spot on a highway near a curve in the road where the barricade would not be seen by an oncoming motorist. The boys would wait to watch an unsuspecting motorist attempt to stop and (usually) crash into the wooden barricade. With saintly bearing, the boys might offer help and understanding.

A stolen lantern might well find its way onto the back of a police car or be hung from a streetlamp. Once a lantern served as a prop for a reenactment of the "midnight ride of Paul Revere" until the "play," which was taking place at 2:00 A.M. in the center of a main street of Big Town, was interrupted when they spotted a police car several blocks away. The boys ran, leaving the lanterns behind, and managed to avoid being apprehended.

Abandoned houses, especially if they were located in out-of-the-way places, were fair game for destruction and spontaneous vandalism. The boys would break windows, remove furniture to the yard and tear it apart, urinate on the walls, and scrawl obscenities inside.

Through all the pranks, drinking, and reckless driving the boys managed miraculously to avoid being stopped by police. Only twice in two years was I aware that they had been stopped by a Big City policeman. Once was for speeding (which they did every time they drove whether they were drunk or sober), and the driver managed to convince the policeman that it was simply an error. The second time they were stopped they had just left a nightclub and were walking through an alley. Aaron stopped to urinate, and the boys began making obscene remarks. A foot patrolman came into the alley, lectured the boys, and sent them home. Before they got to their car, one began talking in a loud voice again. The policeman, who had followed them down the alley, arrested this boy for disturbing the peace and took him to the police station, where the other Saints gathered. After paying a five-dollar fine, and being assured there would be no permanent record of the arrest, the boy was released.

The boys felt a spirit of frivolity and fun in their escapades. They did not view what they were engaged in as "delinquency," though it surely was by any reasonable definition of that word. They simply saw themselves as having a little fun, and who, they would ask, was really hurt by it? The answer had to be no one, although this fact remains one of the most difficult things to explain about the gang's behavior. Unlikely though it seems, in two years of drinking, driving, carousing, and vandalism, no one was seriously injured as a result of the Saints' activities.

The Saints in School

The Saints were highly successful in school. As a whole, the group maintained a B average, and two of the boys maintained close to straight-A averages. Almost all of the boys were popular, and many of them held school offices. One was vice president of the student body one year. Six of the boys played on athletic teams.

At the end of their senior year, the student body selected ten seniors for special recognition as the "school wheels"; four of the ten were Saints. Teachers and school officials saw no problem with any of these boys and anticipated that they would all "make something of themselves."

It is surprising that the boys managed to maintain this impression in view of their actual behavior in school. Their technique for covering truancy was so successful that teachers did not even realize they were absent from school much of the time. Occasionally, of course, the system would backfire, and then the boy was on his own. A boy who was caught would be most contrite, plead guilty, and ask for mercy, which he inevitably got.

Cheating on examinations was rampant, even to the point of not just looking at one another's papers but orally communicating answers. Since none of the group studied, and since they were primarily dependent on one another for help, it is surprising that grades were so high. Teachers contributed to the deception in their admitted inclination to give these boys (and presumably others like them) the benefit of the doubt. When asked how the boys did in school, and when pressed on specific examinations or about particular students, teachers might admit that they were disappointed in the student's performance, but they would quickly add that they "knew he was capable of doing better," so they would give him a higher grade than he had actually earned. How often this happened is impossible to know. During the time that I observed the group, I never saw any of the boys take homework home. Teachers must have been "understanding" very regularly.

One boy who failed to keep up with the gang's generally good performance was Jerry, who had a C average in his junior year and who experienced disaster the next year and failed to graduate. Jerry had always been a little more nonchalant than the others about the liberties he took in school. Rather than waiting for someone to come get him from class, he would offer his own excuse and leave. Although he probably did not miss any more classes than most of the others in the group, he did not take the requisite pains to cover his absences. Jerry was the only Saint whom I ever heard talk back to a teacher. Although teachers often called him a "cutup" or a "smart kid," they never referred to him as a troublemaker or as a kid headed for trouble. It seems likely, then, that

Jerry's mediocre performance his junior year and his failure his senior year were consequences of his not playing the game the proper way (possibly because he was disturbed by his parents' divorce). His teachers regarded him as "immature" and not quite ready to get out of high school.

The Police and the Saints

The local police saw the Saints as good boys who were among the youth leaders of the community. Rarely, the boys might be stopped in town for speeding or for running a stop sign. When this happened the boys were always polite and contrite, and they asked to be forgiven, and as in school, they received the forgiveness they asked for. None ever received a ticket or was taken into the precinct by the local police.

The situation in Big City, where the boys engaged in most of their delinquent behavior, was only slightly different. The police there did not know the boys at all, although occasionally the boys were stopped by a patrolman. Once they were caught taking a lantern from a construction site. Another time they were stopped for running a stop sign, and on several occasions they were stopped for speeding. Their behavior was as before: contrite, polite, and penitent. The urban police, like the local police, accepted their demeanor as sincere. More important, the urban police were convinced that these were good boys just out for a lark.

The Roughnecks

The Roughnecks in the Community

Hanibal townspeople never perceived the Saints' high level of delinquency. They were good boys who just went in for an occasional prank. After all, they were well dressed and well mannered, and they had nice cars. The Roughnecks were a different story. Although the two gangs of boys were the same age, and both groups engaged in an equal amount of wild-oat sowing, everyone agreed that the not-so-well-dressed, not-so-well-mannered, not-so-rich boys were heading for trouble. As one townsperson put it, "You can see the gang members at the drugstore night after night, leaning against the storefront (sometimes drunk) or slouching around inside buying cokes, reading magazines, and probably stealing old Mr. Wall blind. When they are outside and girls walk by, even respectable girls, they make suggestive remarks. Sometimes their remarks are downright lewd."

For the community, the real indication that these kids were in for trouble was that they were constantly involved with the police. Some of them had been picked up for stealing, mostly small stuff, "but still, it's stealing small stuff that leads to big-time crimes. Too bad," people said. "Too bad that these boys couldn't behave like the other kids in town; stay out of trouble, be polite to adults, and look to their future."

The community's impression of the degree to which this group of six boys (ranging in age from sixteen to nineteen) engaged in delinquency was somewhat distorted. In some ways the gang was more delinquent than the community thought; in other ways they were less.

The groups' fighting was fairly, readily, and accurately perceived by almost everyone. At least once a month, the boys would get into some sort of fight, although most fights were scraps between members of the group or involved only one member of the group and some peripheral hanger-on. Only three times in the two-year observation period did the group fight as a unit: once against a gang from across town, once against two black youths, and once against a group of boys from another school. For the first two fights the group went out "looking for trouble," and they found it both times. The third fight followed a football game and began spontaneously with an argument on the football field between one of the Roughnecks and a member of the opposition's football team.

Jack had a particular propensity for fighting and was involved in most of the brawls. He was a prime mover of the escalation of arguments into fights.

The community was not aware of a Roughneck activity more serious than fighting: theft. Although almost everyone was aware that the boys occasionally stole things, they did not realize the extent of the activity. The Roughnecks frequently engaged in petty stealing. Sometimes they stole as a group and coordinated their efforts; other times they stole in pairs. Rarely did they steal alone.

What they stole ranged from very small things like paperback books, comics, and ballpoint pens to expensive items like watches.

Where they stole from also varied from time to time. The gang would go through a period of systematically lifting items from automobiles or school lockers. Types of thievery varied with the whim of the gang, but though some forms of thievery were more profitable than others, all thefts were for profit, not just thrills.

Roughnecks siphoned gasoline from cars whenever they had access to an automobile, which was not very often. Unlike the Saints, who owned their own cars, the Roughnecks had to borrow their parents' cars, which they could do only eight or nine times a year. The boys claimed to have stolen cars for joyrides from time to time.

Ron committed the most serious of the group's offenses. With an associate who was never identified, Ron attempted to burglarize a gasoline station. (Although this station had been robbed twice previously in the same month, Ron denied any involvement in either of the other thefts.) When Ron and his accomplice approached the station, the owner was hiding in the bushes beside it. He fired both barrels of a double-barreled shotgun at the boys. Ron was severely injured; the other boy ran away and was never caught. Though he remained in critical condition for several months, Ron finally recovered and served six months of the following year in reform school. Upon release from reform school, Ron was put back a grade in school. He dropped out of the Roughnecks and began running around with a different gang of boys. The Roughnecks considered Ron's new associates as "nerds," and they were apparently less delinquent than the Roughnecks. During the following year, Ron had no more trouble with the police.

The third of the types of delinquency the Roughnecks engaged in was drinking. Although community members perceived that this gang of boys was delinquent, they mistakenly believed that their illegal activities were primarily drinking, fighting, and harassing passersby. In fact, however, drinking was limited among the gang members (although it did occur), and theft was much more prevalent than anyone realized.

Drinking would doubtless have been more prevalent had the boys had ready access to liquor. Since they rarely had automobiles at their disposal they could not travel very far, and the bars in town would not serve them. Most of the boys had little money, and this, too, inhibited their purchase of alcohol. Their major source of liquor was a local drunk who would buy them a fifth if they would give him enough extra to buy himself a pint of whiskey or a bottle of wine.

The community's perception that they drank frequently stemmed from the fact that drinking was the most obvious delinquency the boys engaged in. When one of the boys had been drinking, even a casual observer seeing him on the corner could tell he was drunk.

The Police and the Roughnecks

There was a high level of mutual distrust and dislike between the Roughnecks and the police. The boys felt very strongly that the police were unfair and corrupt, and there was some evidence that they were correct.

The main source of the boys' dislike for the police was undoubtedly the fact that the police would sporadically harass the group. From the boys' standpoint, this occasional enforcement of the law was whimsical and uncalled-for. It made no sense to them that the police would threaten them with arrest for loitering on a corner when the night before they had been out siphoning gasoline from cars and the police had been nowhere in sight. The boys saw the police as stupid, on the one hand, for not being where they should have been and catching them in a serious offense, and as unfair, on the other, for trumping up "loitering" charges against them.

The police saw the situation quite differently. They knew, with all the confidence necessary to be a policeman, that these boys were engaged in criminal activities. They knew this partly from occasionally catching them, mostly from circumstantial evidence ("the boys were around when those tires were slashed"), and partly because the police shared the view of the community in general that this was a bad bunch of boys. The best the police could hope to do was to be sensitive to the fact that these boys were engaged in illegal acts and to arrest them whenever there was any evidence that they had been involved. Whether or not the boys had in fact committed a particular act in a particular way was not especially important. The police had a broader view: Their job was to stamp out these kids' crimes; their tactics were not as important as the end result.

Over the period that the group was under observation, each member was arrested at least once. Several of the boys were arrested a number of times and spent at least one night in jail. Although most were never taken to court, two of the boys were sentenced to six months' incarceration in reform schools.

The Roughnecks in School

The Roughnecks were not particularly disruptive in school. During school hours they did not all hang around together; instead, they tended to spend most of their time with one or two other members of the gang who were their special buddies. Although every member of the gang attempted to avoid school as much as possible, they were not particularly successful in evading it, and most of them attended school with surprising regularity. They considered school a burden—something to be gotten through with a minimum of conflict. If they were "bugged" by a particular teacher, it could lead to trouble. One of the boys, Al, once threatened to beat up a teacher and, according to the other boys, the teacher hid under a desk to escape him.

Teachers, like the general community, saw the boys as heading for trouble and as being uninterested in making something of themselves. They also saw some of the boys as being incapable of meeting the academic standards of the school. Most of the teachers expressed concern for this group of boys and were willing to pass them despite poor performance, believing that failing them would only aggravate the problem.

Academically, the group of boys had an average just slightly above C. No one in the group failed any of their grades, and no one had better than a C average. They were very consistent in their achievement or, at least, the teachers were consistent in their perception of the boys' achievement.

Two of the boys were good football players. Herb was acknowledged to be the best player in the school, and Jack was almost as good. Both boys were criticized for their failure to abide by training rules, for refusing to come to practice as often as they should, and for not playing their best during practice. Apparently what they lacked in sportsmanship they made up for in skill, and they played every game no matter how poorly they had performed in practice or how many practice sessions they had missed.

Two Questions

Why did the community, the school, and the police react to the Saints as though they were good, upstanding, nondelinquent youths with bright futures but to the Roughnecks as though they were tough young criminals headed for trouble? Why did the Roughnecks and the Saints in fact have quite different careers after high school—careers that by and large lived up to the expectations of the community?

The most obvious explanation for the differences in the community's and the law enforcement agencies' reactions to the two gangs is that one group of boys was "more delinquent" than the other. But which group *was* "more delinquent"? The answer to this question will partly determine the difference in responses to these groups by the members of the community and, particularly, by law enforcement and school officials.

In the sheer number of illegal acts, the Saints were the more delinquent. They were truant from school for at least part of the day almost every day of the week. In addition, they drank and committed vandalism surprisingly regularly. The Roughnecks, in contrast, engaged only sporadically in delinquent episodes, and although these episodes were frequent, they certainly did not occur on a daily or even a weekly basis.

The difference in frequency of offenses was probably caused by the Roughnecks' inability to obtain liquor or to manipulate legitimate excuses to get out of school. Since the Roughnecks had less money than the Saints and since teachers carefully supervised their school activities, the Roughnecks' misdeeds were not nearly as frequent as the Saints' even though their hearts may have been as black.

There are really no clear-cut criteria by which to measure qualitative differences in antisocial behavior. The most important dimension of the difference is generally referred to as the "seriousness" of the offenses.

If seriousness encompasses the relative economic costs of delinquent acts, then some assessments can be made. The Roughnecks probably stole an average of about five dollars' worth of goods a week. Some weeks the figure was considerably higher, but these times must be balanced against long periods when almost nothing was stolen.

The Saints were more continuously engaged in delinquency, but for the most part their acts were not costly to property. Only their vandalism and occasional theft of gasoline caused someone economic loss. Perhaps once or twice a month they would siphon a tankful of gas. They also stole such costly items as street signs, construction lanterns, and the like. Nevertheless, the cost of all of this together probably did not quite come to five dollars a week, partly because they abandoned much of the stolen equipment, and it was presumably recovered. The difference in cost of stolen property between the two groups was trivial, but the Roughnecks probably had a slightly more expensive set of activities than did the Saints.

Another facet of seriousness is potential threat of physical harm, either to members of the community or to the boys themselves. The Roughnecks were more prone to physical violence; they not only welcomed an opportunity to fight, they went seeking it. In addition, they fought among themselves frequently. Although the fighting never included deadly weapons, it was still a menace, however minor, to the physical safety of those involved.

The Saints never fought. They avoided physical conflict both inside and outside the group. At the same time, though, the Saints endangered their own and other people's lives almost every time they drove a car, and especially if they had been drinking. Sober, their driving was risky; under the influence of alcohol it was horrendous. In addition, the Saints' pranks endangered the lives of others: Street excavations left unmarked were a very serious hazard.

Evaluating the relative seriousness of the two gangs' activities is difficult. The community reacted as though the Roughnecks' behavior was a problem, and they reacted as though the Saints' behavior was not. But the community members and the police were ignorant of the wide array of delinquent acts the Saints indulged in. Although concerned citizens were unaware of much of the Roughnecks' behavior as well, they were much better informed about the Roughnecks' involvement in delinquency than they were about the Saints'.

Visibility

The two gangs were treated differently partly because one gang's delinquent behavior was far more visible than the other's. This differential visibility was a direct function of the social class of their families. The Saints had access to automobiles and were able to remove themselves from the community's sight. Even for something as innocuous as having a milk shake after school, the Saints stayed away from the mainstream of community life. Lacking transportation, the Roughnecks could not make it to the edge of town. The center of town was the only practical place for them to meet, since without automobiles any noncentral meeting place put an undue hardship on some members. Of necessity, the Roughnecks congregated in a crowded area that everyone in the community, including teachers and police officers, passed frequently. Everyone could easily see the Roughnecks hanging around the drugstore.

The Roughnecks, of course, made themselves even more visible by making remarks to passersby and by occasionally getting into fights on the corner. Meanwhile, the Saints were just as regularly either at the café at one edge of town or in the pool hall at the other edge of town. Without particularly realizing that they were making themselves inconspicuous, the Saints were nonetheless able to hide their time wasting. Not only were they removed from the mainstream of traffic, but they were almost always inside a building.

The Saints were also relatively invisible on their escapades, since they left Hanibal and traveled to Big City. Here, too, they were mobile, roaming the city, rarely going to the same area twice.

Demeanor

Members of the two groups also responded differently to outside intervention in their activities. If one of the Saints was confronted by an accusing policeman his demeanor was apologetic and penitent, even if he felt he was truly innocent of a wrongdoing. A Roughneck's attitude was almost the polar opposite: When confronted by a threatening adult authority, even one trying to be pleasant, the Roughneck's hostility and disdain were clearly observable. Sometimes he might attempt to put on a veneer of respect, but it was thin and was not accepted as sincere by the authority.

School was no different from the community at large. The Saints could manipulate the system by feigning compliance with the school norms. Their access to cars at school meant that once free from the immediate sight of teachers, the boys could disappear rapidly. They always planned their escape carefully to make sure no administrator or teacher was nearby when they left. A Roughneck who wished to escape for a few hours was in a bind. If he could get free from class, downtown was still a mile away, and even if he made it there, he was still very visible. The Roughnecks were almost certain to be detected in truancy, whereas the Saints enjoyed almost complete immunity from sanctions.

Bias

Community members were not aware of the Saints' transgressions, but even if the Saints had been less discreet their favorite delinquencies would have been perceived as less serious than those of the Roughnecks.

In the eyes of the police and of school officials, a boy who drinks in an alley and stands intoxicated on the street corner, who steals a paperback from a store, or who associates with someone who has committed a burglary is a delinquent. A boy who gets drunk in a nightclub or tavern, even if he drives around afterwards in a car, is perceived as someone who has made a mistake. Stealing a lantern from a construction site is not perceived as indicating serious delinquency, but shoplifting a pair of gloves from a department store is.

In other words, there is a built-in class bias in the definition of what constitutes "serious" delinquency. Just as driving under the influence is treated by law enforcement agencies with greater leniency than possession of illegal drugs (see Chapter 4), the delinquencies available to upper-middle-class youths are seen as less serious than those available to lower-class youths. Why this is so is best explained by the way the law enforcement system is organized and by who has the power to affect it.

The Organization of Policing

Differences in the visibility and demeanor of the Saints and the Roughnecks and bias by the community, including the police, account for the day-to-day operations of the police. Why do these surface variables operate as they do? Why did the police choose to disregard the Saints' delinquencies while breathing down the necks of the Roughnecks?

The answer lies in the class structure of U.S. society and the control of legal institutions by those at the top of the class structure.

Put quite simply, if the police treat middle- upper-class delinquents (or cocaine-snorting college students) the same way they treat lower-class delinquents (or black, ghetto crack users), they are asking for trouble from people in power. If, on the other hand, they focus their law enforcement efforts on the lower classes, they are praised and supported by "the community," that is, by the middle- and upper-class white community.

There is no conscious conspiracy to arrest and imprison the lower classes for acts that are no more harmful than the crimes of the middle and upper classes. There is no community leader telling the police to look on street corners and in the ghettos for crime. The law does not dictate that the demeanor of lower-class youths bespeaks future criminality and that of upper-middle-class youths promises future success. Rather, the decisions of the police and teachers grow from their experience: experience with irate and influential upper-middle-class parents insisting that their son's vandalism was simply a prank and his drunkenness only a momentary "sowing of wild oats" and experience with cooperative or indifferent, powerless lower-class parents acquiescing to the law's definition of their son's behavior.

As I pointed out in Chapter 3, members of organizations are rewarded for acts that minimize strain and maximize gains for the organization. Police who arrest poor kids for stealing bicycles or selling drugs are doing a good job and are promoted. Police who arrest upper-middle-class kids for being truant and hanging out in pool halls create strains that no police chief wants. It does not take many encounters with irate parents and their high-priced lawyers for the police to learn to ignore the drug dealing on college campuses or the vandalism of middle-class kids. It just makes organizational sense to look for crime in the ghetto rather than the suburbs and to send middle-class kids home with a warning rather than arresting them and facing the inevitable criticism of superiors.

As Adults

Adult Careers of the Saints

The community's confidence in the potential of the Saints and the Roughnecks was apparently justified. If anything, the community members underestimated the degree to which these youngsters would turn out "good" and "bad."

Seven of the eight members of the Saints went on to college immediately after high school. Five of the boys graduated from college in four years. The sixth finished college after two years in the army, and the seventh spent four years in the air force before returning to college and receiving a B.A. degree. Of these seven college graduates, three went on to professional or postgraduate degrees. One finished law school and for a while was active in state politics, one finished medical school and is practicing near Hanibal, and another completed a Ph.D. in history and is teaching at a small state university. The other four college graduates entered submanagerial, managerial, or executive training positions with larger firms immediately upon graduation, and though they have changed firms from time to time, three of the four have remained in managerial positions throughout their careers. The fourth, Charles, went to work for the government for a period before quitting to sell real estate.

The only Saint who did not complete college was Jerry. Jerry failed to graduate from high school with the other Saints. During his second senior year, after the other Saints had gone on to college, Jerry began to hang around with what several teachers described as a "rough crowd." At the end of his second senior year, when he did graduate from high school, Jerry took a job as a used-car salesman, got married, and quickly had a child. Although he made several abortive attempts to go to college by attending night school, ten years after he graduated from high school Jerry was unemployed and had been living on unemployment for almost a year. His wife worked as a waitress.

Adult Careers of the Roughnecks

Some of the Roughnecks lived up to community expectations, some did not. A number of them had indeed been headed for trouble.

Jack and Herb were the athletes among the Roughnecks, and their athletic prowess paid off handsomely. Both boys received unsolicited athletic scholarships to college. After Herb received his scholarship (near the end of his senior year), he did an about-face. His demeanor became very similar to that of the Saints. Although he remained a member in good standing of the Roughnecks, he stopped participating in most of their activities and did not hang on the corner with them as often. When I met him in the parking lot of a shopping center the summer after high school graduation he was dressed in a suit and tie. He came up to me and shook my hand (which would have been unheard of for him only a few months earlier), took me to his car, and introduced me to his mother. Suddenly Herb was the "gentleman" that the college he would be attending expected their students to be.

Jack did not change. If anything, he became more prone to fighting. He even made excuses for accepting the scholarship. He told the other gang members that the school had guaranteed him a C average if he would come to play football, which seems far-fetched even in this day of highly competitive recruiting. During the summer after graduation from high school, Jack attempted to commit suicide by jumping from a tall building. The jump would certainly have killed most people trying it, but Jack survived. He entered college in the fall and played four years of football.

Jack and Herb graduated in four years, and both are teaching and coaching in high schools. Jack is the vice principal of his high school. They are married and have stable families. Jack appears to have a more prestigious position in the community than does Herb, though both are well respected and secure in their positions.

Two of the boys never finished high school. Tommy left at the end of his junior year and went to another state. That summer he was arrested and placed on probation on a manslaughter charge. Three years later he was arrested for murder; he pleaded guilty to second-degree murder and served twelve years of a thirty-year sentence in the state penitentiary before being released.

Al, the other boy who did not finish high school, also moved to another state in his senior year. When Al was twenty-four he was accused of murdering a man in a fight. He served fourteen years of a life sentence in a state penitentiary for first degree murder. While he was in prison he got into a fight and was stabbed, and as a result he was paralyzed from the waist down. Upon release from prison Al purchased a small grocery store, which he ran successfully until his death.

Wes is a small-time gambler. He finished high school and "bummed around." After several years he made contact with a bookmaker who employed him as a runner. Later he acquired his own area and has been working it ever since. His position among the bookmakers is almost identical to the position he had in the gang: He is always around, but no one is really aware of him. He makes no trouble, and he does not get into any. Steady, reliable, capable of keeping his mouth closed, he plays the game by the rules, even though the game is an illegal one.

That leaves only Ron. Some of his former friends reported that they had heard he was "driving a truck up north," but I was unable to find him.

Labeling and the Self-Fulfilling Prophecy

The community treated the Roughnecks as if they were boys in trouble, and the boys agreed with that diagnosis. Their pattern of deviance was reinforced, and it became increasingly unlikely that they would break away from that pattern. Once the boys acquired an image of themselves as deviants, they selected new friends who affirmed that self-image. As that self-conception became more firmly entrenched, they also became willing to try new and more-extreme deviances. With their growing alienation came freer expression of disrespect and hostility for representatives of the legitimate society. This disrespect increased the community's negativism, perpetuating the entire process of commitment to deviance. Lack of commitment to deviance can be reinforced and developed the same way. In either case, the process will perpetuate itself unless some event (like a scholarship to college or a sudden failure) external to the established relationship intervenes. For two of the Roughnecks (Herb and Jack), receiving college athletic scholarships created new relations and led to a break with their established patterns of deviance.

One of the Saints (Jerry) also suffered significant changes in his interpersonal relationships. His parents' divorce and his failure to graduate from high school led to his being held back in school for a year and losing his place among the Saints, which had sufficient impact on him to alter his self-image and virtually to assure that he would not go on to college as his peers had. Although the experiments of life can rarely be reversed, it seems probable that if Jerry had not experienced the "special consideration" of his teachers, which kept him from graduating with his peers, he too would have "become something." For Herb and Jack, outside intervention and labeling worked in a way opposite to the way it did for Jerry.

Selective perception and labeling: The discovery, processing, and punishing of some kinds of criminality and not others means that visible, poor, nonmobile, outspoken, undiplomatic, "tough" kids will be noticed, whether their actions are seriously delinquent or not. Other kids, who establish a reputation for being bright (even if underachieving), reasonably polite, and involved in respectable activities and who are mobile and monied, will be invisible when they deviate from sanctioned activities. They will sow their wild oats, perhaps even more widely and thickly than their lower-class cohorts, but they will not be noticed. After adolescence, most will follow the expected path, settling into the ways of the middle class, remembering fondly the delinquent but unnoticed flings of their youth. The Roughnecks, and others like them, may turn around, too. It is more likely, however, that their noticeable deviance and the reaction to it will have been so reinforced by police and community that their lives will be effectively channeled into careers consistent with the self-image they developed in adolescence.

The patterns of deviance established in adolescence and the reaction of significant actors in the community may well be reproduced in adulthood. The Saints apparently became law-abiding, successful upper-middle-class adults. But were they so law-abiding?

The Saint who became a lawyer had to leave the state where he was practicing law because of a pending lawsuit alleging criminal violation of trust. The suit was dropped after he paid a substantial amount of money to the plaintiff. The lawsuit alleged not only a violation of trust but complicity with organized crime figures. He relocated his practice to Atlantic City, New Jersey, where, one of his former classmates told me, he works closely with organized crime figures. I have no way at this time of verifying this information.

Did the Saint who became a medical doctor or those who work for corporations commit criminal acts? Did they smoke pot or snort cocaine as adults? Were they involved in price fixing, insider trading, or tax evasion? When I interviewed them recently and raised these questions I was met only with laughter and the admission, as one put it, "Well, maybe a little pot occasionally and of

BOX 5.1 Commentary: What a Prison Sentence Really Means

Jeff Goodman

Minneapolis Star-Tribune, December 30, 1998, B12

When I was sent to prison, the judge mentioned just the length of my sentence. Had he included the entire scope of my punishment, he may have said it differently:

"Mr. Goodman, I sentence you to take responsibility for every social ill—past, present, and future. Each time America runs out of foreign enemies, it apparently turns on itself to find more. By way of media, politics, and indifference, people who break the law, good law or bad, become those enemies and are then responsible for every social malady. Whether this is logical,

(continues)

course tax evasion." It is impossible to say how criminal the Saints were as adults, for although I have kept in contact with some of them over the years, the closeness we shared when they were teenagers has eroded with time. They also can be expected to be considerably more circumspect about their adult crimes than they were about their juvenile "games."

Power's prophylactic ability to deflect scrutiny, to inhibit the detection of criminal acts, or to prevent one from being labeled criminal, which covered the Saints as adolescents, may well be protecting them as adults. As we shall see in the chapters that follow, criminal behavior exists among people in high as well as low places. Those in low places, like the Roughnecks, are much more likely to be arrested and imprisoned, whereas people in high places, like the Saints, usually avoid paying such a high price for their crimes.

The most important question this study of the Roughnecks and the Saints raises is this: How many poor young men—black, brown, and white—incarcerated for minor offenses, would be in college today instead of prison had they been treated by the police and the community the way the Saints were treated? How many Saints would be in prison instead of going on to college had they been treated as were the Roughnecks? We cannot answer this question. But labeling, stigma, and negative self-images have a powerful impact in determining who we are and what we become. (See Box 5.1.) One lesson is inescapable: The less the intervention in the minor crimes of juveniles, the better off they and society will be.

BOX 5.1 *(continued)*

you are the culprit.

"You are sentenced to live in a maladaptive, alien environment that defies description. You'll be stripped of your work skills, your self-worth and your humanity while at the same time [you will] face the daily threat of assault, rape, false accusations, and unjustified punishment. You will live like this for seven years. If you manage to reenter society as a productive person, some will say prison was just what you needed. If not, others will say, 'I told you so.'

"Because of counterproductive prison policies, you are sentenced to live in a world of cruelty and indifference that engenders the very behavior it purports to alleviate. If you share this with those outside of the prison system, you will be called a liar; most won't believe that millions are spent on the proliferation of facilities that perpetuate harm, not repair it.

"You are sentenced to consume $150,000 in taxpayer dollars for your prison stay. While lawmakers cite the ever-growing cost of incarceration as a public necessity, you will learn that 10 percent of that amount goes towards your daily needs, while the other 90 percent pays for a bloated prison bureaucracy immune from any cost-benefit analysis. These tax dollars will be siphoned from school programs, child care and job training, all of which do make our communities healthy and safe and save millions in the process. Despite the media frenzy that portrays society as seething with crime, you'll learn that relatively few prisoners represent a danger to our communities; we're mad at most felons, not scared of them. So you'll wonder why the majority of prisoners aren't on home arrest, a logical move that would save millions of dollars and obviate the need for more prisons.

"Practical education programs, universally proven to drastically reduce recidivism, will be almost nonexistent. In fact, you will be disciplined for possessing more than 10 books. Therefore, you will live in an environment where recidivism is tacitly encouraged, a fact not lost on those who want to run prisons for profit.

"It is true that there are some counseling programs in prison and some people will benefit from them. Yet, if you attempt to describe the futility of a therapeutic environment placed within an atmosphere replete with dehumanizing policies, you will be told that your intentions are distorted and without merit.

"You are sentenced to bear the wrath of a misinformed society. While you're experiencing everything I just said, you will be told how easy you have it. The media will find your Christmas meal more newsworthy than the damage caused by lawmakers who jostle for the next 'get tough' policy at the expense of society's well-being. Your privilege to have this once-a-year meal will be presented as so outrageous, a debate will ensue over which

(continues)

BOX 5.1 *(continued)*

'luxury' to take away next. Politicians will focus on violent sociopaths and pronounce their horrific crimes as a yardstick to measure the innate danger and incorrigibility of all lawbreakers, including you.

"Finally, as perhaps the most perverse component of your sentence, I hereby prohibit society from ever listening to you. Your comments on crime and punishment will be ignored. You, as well as others, will see the big picture, but few will care about the politics of crime and its role in our growing prison population. You will know that most prisoners are guilty of breaking the law, but only a few need to be separated from society. You will know that it is the reporting and sensationalism of crime that has skyrocketed, not crime itself. Unfortunately, though you will one day return to society with firsthand knowledge of our prison system, few will care; most see only the door leading into prison, not the one leading out.

"Therefore, if your opinion ever gets printed in a newspaper, you will not only be perceived as just another lawbreaker unable to accept the consequences of his actions, but of being manipulative as well. Society will know this to be so because you once broke the law.

"You are hereby sentenced to be a messenger whose message will be forever perceived as tainted, self-serving and disingenuous, regardless of its veracity and accuracy.

"No one will believe you.

"You have been sentenced to be a criminal."

Note

1. All the names in this chapter, including the name of the high school, are pseudonyms.

Part 3

Implications

Chapter Six

Trading Textbooks for Prison Cells

In his 1997 State of the Union address President Clinton called for an infusion of federal funds "to ensure that all Americans have the best education in the world." It was typical political rhetoric. At the same time, he called for vast increases in expenditures on crime control. The contradiction was easy to spot, and no one should have been surprised that it was education, not crime control, that took the hit when the president signed the final budget in 1998. Clinton repeated his call for substantial increases in education expenditures in 1999, and he called for similar increases for crime control. There is nothing to indicate that the year 2000 will not be a repeat of 1998.

Even if Clinton had delivered on his promise to give federal priority to education, it would not make up for the fact that on the state and local level crime control expenditures are given priority over educational expenditures. Most of the educational costs for elementary and secondary schools are born by municipal and county governments. Higher education costs (colleges and universities) are paid for mainly at the state level. The federal government's contribution is in any event minimal.

In 1990 the nation's criminal justice system employed nearly 2 million people and cost the taxpayers more than $70 billion. It is estimated that by the year 2002 the criminal justice system will cost more than $200 billion. Between 1973 and 1993 expenditures nationwide on corrections (prison building, maintenance, and parole) increased by 1,200 percent; in the same period, expenditures on higher education increased by only 419 percent.[1] Total capital outlay increased 326 percent for corrections and 159 percent for higher education between 1980 and 1990. Whereas in 1994 higher education was financed by $3.4 billion in state bonds and corrections by $1.6 billion, in 1995 the relative position was reversed: Corrections were funded by approximately $2.6 billion in state bonds and higher education received approximately $2.5 billion.

The relative decrease in tax revenues going to colleges and universities has forced an increase in tuition at all public higher education institutions. These increases, in turn, place an added burden on students from poorer families, as they are forced to either forego higher education or work extensively to pay for it. Thus the role of higher education as an "equalizer of opportunity" is undermined. Indeed, higher education becomes instead a mechanism for reinforcing and maintaining the class structure. The persistence of a large class of poor people, in turn, guarantees a constant supply of people to be arrested and incarcerated.

The shifting in funding priorities, from higher education compared to corrections, is repeated at the state, county, and municipal government levels, where for the first time in U.S. history more money is being spent on criminal justice than on primary and secondary education. Education is being sacrificed on the altar of the criminal justice–industrial complex. State expenditures showed the largest increase, rising more than twelvefold from per capita expenditures on police and corrections of $8 in 1969 to $100 in 1992. State spending on corrections increased most dramatically, increasing by 95 percent whereas state spending on higher education (colleges and universities) decreased by 6 percent. Between 1982 and 1993 there was a 129 percent increase in the number of correctional officers but an increase of only 28.5 percent in the number of instructional faculty in public higher education.[2] (See Figure 6.1.)

State government expenditure for building prisons increased 593 percent in actual dollars, and increases in state spending on higher education are disproportionately low.[3] As the Center for the Study of the States notes, "higher education is the biggest loser in the state budget battles of the early 1990s."[4] Indeed, increases in state expenditures on corrections are often directly proportional to de-

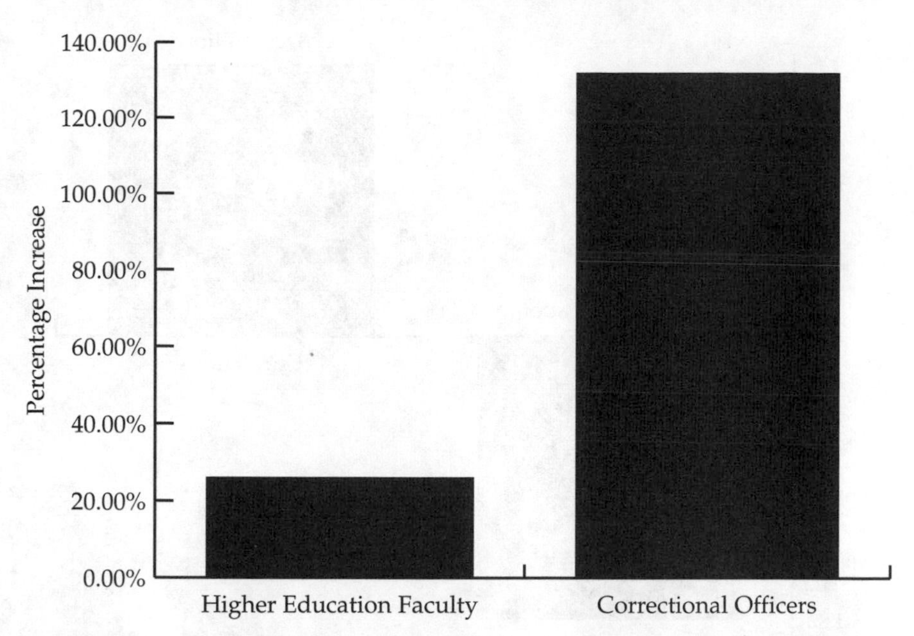

FIGURE 6.1 Percentage Increase of Correctional Officers Versus Public Higher Education Faculty, 1982–1993

SOURCE: U.S. Department of Education, *Digest of Education Statistics 1996* (Washington, D.C.: National Center for Education Statistics, 1996), Table 220; American Correctional Association, Table: "Correctional Officers in Adult Systems" (Lanham, Md.: ACA).

creases in expenditures on education: Between 1994 and 1995 the total state bond fund expenditures for education decreased by $954 million while the total state bond fund expenditures for corrections increased by $926 million. (See Figure 6.2.) California, whose higher education system was once the envy of every other state, now is "envied" by correctional officers and criminal justice employees, who saw an increase of more than 25,000 employees in the Department of Corrections workforce between 1984 and 1994; at the same time, there was a decline of more than 8,000 employees in higher education.[5]

The number of police officers and civilian employees in law enforcement in the United States doubled between 1980 and 1992, and in 1994 the Senate passed and President Clinton signed into law the most expensive federal crime bill in history. The Violent Crime Control and Law Enforcement Act provided state and municipal governments with $30 billion to add 100,000 new police of-

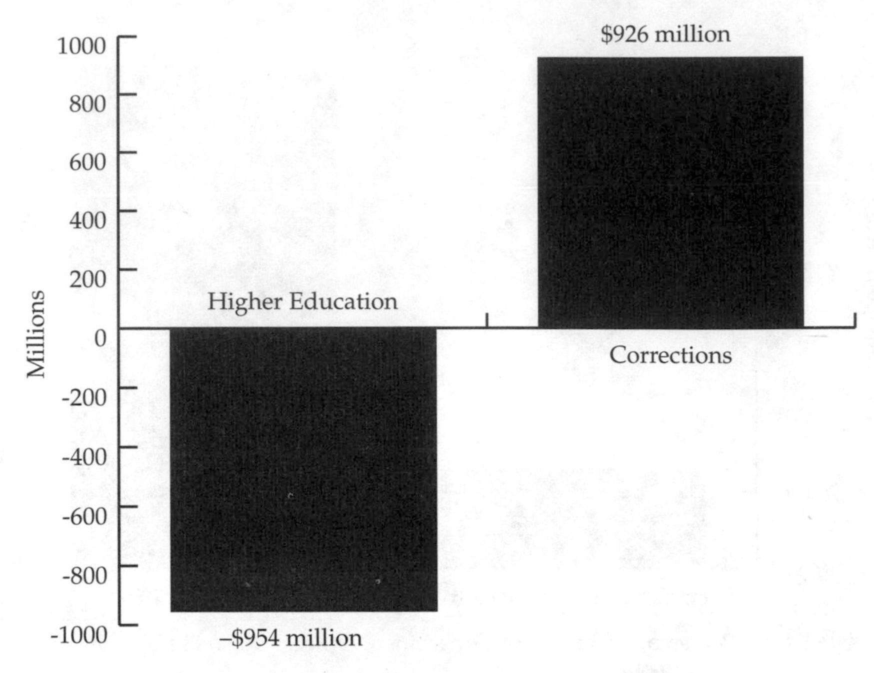

FIGURE 6.2 Building Prisons at the Expense of Colleges: The Dollar-for-Dollar Tradeoff, 1994–1995

SOURCE: National Association of State Budget Officers (NASBO), *1995 State Expenditures Report* (Washington, D.C.: NASBO, April 1996), 77, Table A-6; 98, Table A-22.

ficers, build prisons, and employ more prison guards. This bill was, of course, lobbied for and strongly supported by correctional officer associations, police trade unions, and private corporations specializing in the prison industry, including building contractors, food suppliers (such as Marriott), and others who profit from increased expenditures on criminal justice. Police and correctional officers unions have become increasingly powerful lobbies. In California, the Correctional Officers Union contributed three times more money to conservative Pete Wilson's gubernatorial campaign than any other group in the state.[6]

The power of police lobbies was demonstrated dramatically in Washington, D.C., when the Congressional Budget Office (CBO) in 1997 concluded from its study of D.C. government expenditures that the number of police officers could safely be reduced: "The

District could cut 1,600 positions [from the municipal police department] and have no fewer cops on the beat . . . we came to the conclusion that the last 1,000 positions [that Congress added to the D.C. budget] were unnecessary." Washington has more police officers per capita than any city in the United States. The Fraternal Order of Police, however, were adamant and vocal in their opposition to the CBO's conclusions. They lobbied furiously to restore the original budget, despite evidence that some police officers were earning more than $150,000 a year in overtime without making any significant number of arrests. In the end, slashes in education funding remained in the budget, but police funds were not cut. The mayor, Marion Barry, had proposed a reduction in the number of police officers or a freeze on hiring new officers; instead, 350 new police officers were added to the force—this in a city where classrooms are overcrowded, the roofs of school buildings leak, books and pencils are in scarce supply, and the school toilets are unusable.

In neighboring Prince Georges County, Maryland, the county executive recommended reducing the number of police officers. The police officers' union hired a public relations firm and ran televisions commercials citing increasing crime rates and accusing the county executive of "handcuffing" the police. The union spent more than $10,000 in one week on television and newspaper advertisements.

Since the presidency of Ronald Reagan, the federal government has increased its allocation of resources for criminal justice without a pause. The War on Drugs, whose 1981 budget was $1 billion, received more than $20 billion in 2000. The government added 700 FBI agents in 1990, an increase of 25 percent. Meanwhile teachers have been fired in cities where students are already suffering from large classes and poor facilities. Cities are forced to lay off teachers, cut salaries of public employees, and reduce expenditures in every category except law enforcement. Florida's state legislature decreased per pupil spending from $3,899 per year in 1989 to $3,870 in 1990. School officials estimated that 4,000–6,000 teachers would be fired as a result of these cuts. In Los Angeles from 1990 to 1991 the Board of Education cut $341 million from its budget. These cuts reduced the use of substitute teachers and eliminated school counselors and after-school programs.

In the wake of the Oklahoma City bombing of a federal building in 1995, President Clinton asked Congress for authorization to add 1,000 more officers to the Bureau of Alcohol, Tobacco, and Firearms, the agency whose shoot-out at Ruby Ridge, Idaho, and the Branch Davidian compound in Waco, Texas, may have instigated the Oklahoma City bombing. In practically the same breath, Clinton proposed drastic cuts in federal programs for the poor and elderly. Programs that provide a safety net for the poor—such as food stamps, Aid for Families with Dependent Children (AFDC), and job training—will be reduced by more than $60 billion between 1995 and 2000. In real dollars the AFDC program's cash contribution to a mother with two children and no outside employment dropped from $7,836 in 1982 to $4,801 in 1991, and was down to $4,101 in 1999. Proposals in Congress to "balance the budget" and "reduce the deficit" focus almost exclusively on cutting Medicare for the elderly, welfare for the poor, job training for the unemployed, despite annually increasing expenditures on police, prisons, and repression.

The Fiscal Costs of Imprisonment

It costs an average of nearly $22,000 a year to keep a person in prison. The cost of alternatives to prison is considerably less: Residential drug treatment programs cost an average of $15,000 a year; intensive probation, $6,500; day treatment centers, $5,000; and outpatient drug treatment programs, only $3,500. When these costs are put in perspective by remembering that drug offenses account for the majority of the increase in incarceration in the 1990s, it is obvious that in purely economic terms sentencing people to prison rather than drug treatment programs is fiscally irresponsible. Prison is by far the most costly of all the alternatives, and it is the least effective in reducing crime. (See Figure 6.3.)

Why?

Virtually everyone who studies or works in the criminal justice system agrees that putting people in prison is costly and ineffective. The prisons are filled with people guilty of what the general public considers "minor offenses"; that is, current policies not only do not

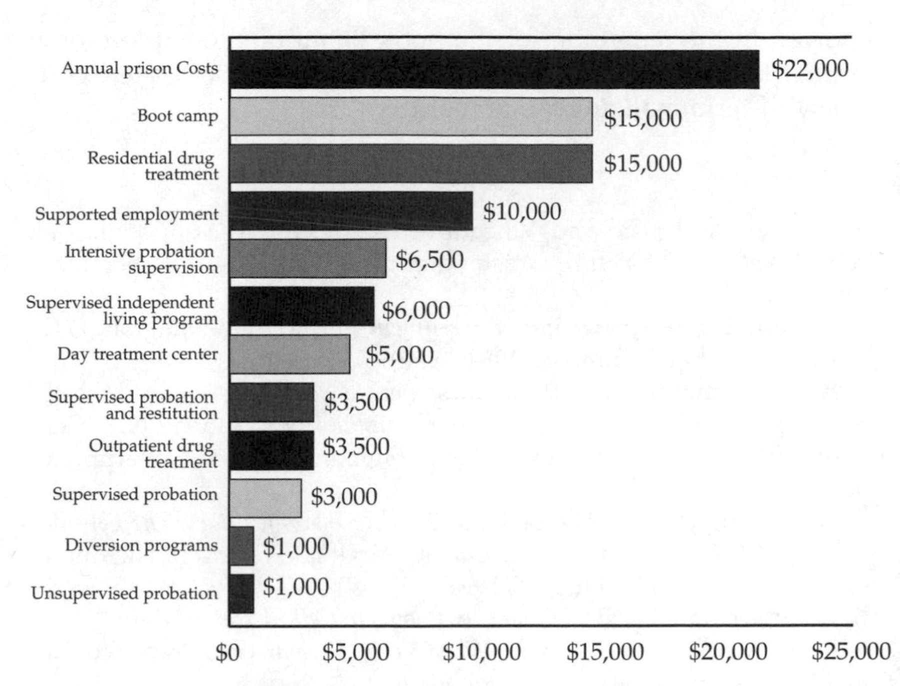

FIGURE 6.3 Cost of Prison Compared to Alternative Sanctions

SOURCE: Donziger, Steven, ed., *The Real War on Crime: Report of the National Criminal Justice Commission* (New York: HarperCollins, 1996), 58.

work, they do not even correspond to public opinion.[7] The question to be asked, then, is why a policy that is irrational, inhumane, costly, and ineffective continues to be pursued?

Some of the answers to this question have been suggested in preceding chapters: The existing system is a consequence of publicizing and exploiting crime to further politics, bureaucratic organizational demands, and media popularity. It is also a mechanism for controlling and repressing a large percentage of the U.S. population that is unemployed and for the foreseeable future unemployable. The fact that this unemployable population is predominantly African American also both reinforces and expresses the ubiquitous racist ideology of U.S. culture.

The imprisonment of large numbers of poor minorities and the shift in emphasis from education and welfare to prisons and criminal justice also hides far more serious harms being done by those in power. In the remainder of the book I continue to explore how criminal law enforcement protects the powerful, and their children, while criminalizing the powerless.

Notes

1. Tara-Jen Ambrosio and Vincent Shiraldi, *From Classrooms to Cell Blocks: A National Perspective* (Washington, D.C.: The Justice Policy Institute, 1997).

2. Bureau of the Census, *State Government Finances* (Washington, D.C.: U.S. Department of Commerce, 1984–1992).

3. Ambrosio and Shiraldi, *From Classrooms to Cell Blocks.*

4. Steve D. Gold, *State Spending Patterns in the 1990s* (Albany, N.Y.: Center for State Studies, Nelson A. Rockefeller Institute of Government, 1995), 17.

5. Noah Baum and Brooke Bedrick, *Trading Books for Bars: The Lopsided Funding Battle Between Prisons and Universities* (San Francisco: The Center on Juvenile and Criminal Justice, 1994).

6. Ambrosio and Shiraldi, *From Classrooms to Cell Blocks*, 19.

7. James Austin and John Irwin, *Who Goes to Prison?* (San Francisco: National Council on Crime and Delinquency).

Chapter Seven

Crime Myths and Smoke Screens

There are sound political, economic, and organizational reasons for creating the myth that to stem the tide of street crimes committed by young black men requires massive expenditures, the expansion of police powers, and the erosion of civil liberties. This myth also serves another function for politicians and law enforcement agencies: Keeping a nation focused on street crimes and the myth of young black men as superpredators is a smoke screen. It deflects criticism from failed social policies that have not effectively dealt with pressing social issues such as poverty and inequalities in race and class.[1] Instead the victims of these failed policies are blamed for the problems, and increasingly repressive measures directed at the victims are implemented and supported at all levels of government, including police on the streets, politicians, and judges all the way to the U.S. Supreme Court.

The myth of street crimes also is a smoke screen behind which far more serious crimes go undetected, are hidden from public view, and are minimally enforced. Crimes of corporations that kill, maim, and cause serious illnesses to hundreds of thousands of Americans every year are scarcely mentioned in the media. Corporate crimes are not recorded by any of the national crime reporting systems. Crimes committed by law enforcement officials, politicians, and the state are also hidden from public scrutiny and, for the most part, go underenforced, unreported, and unpunished.

Police Crimes

Police Brutality and Misfeasance

The end of the twentieth century was reminiscent of the end of the nineteenth century: Both landmark historical moments were punctuated by massive scandals exposing police corruption and brutality. In the early 1900s the exposés of newspaper reporters like Lincoln Stephens documented widespread graft and corruption in big-city police departments.[2] Today it is the occasional amateur videotape and the testimony of police officers plea-bargaining to avoid long prison sentences that have opened a Pandora's box of corruption and brutality, directed, of course, against African American and Latino minorities in poor sections of our cities.

Rafael Perez of the Los Angeles Police Department was caught stealing six pounds of cocaine from a police locker. To cut a deal with the prosecutor for a less severe penalty, Perez agreed to testify to a host of criminal offenses committed by Los Angeles officers that he witnessed during his time as an officer on the special Ramparts antigang unit of the LAPD. In some 2,000 pages of riveting testimony, Perez detailed a slew of crimes committed by him and his fellow police officers. He testified that officers routinely lied in their reports and court testimony (they called themselves the "liars' club") in order to get convictions. They planted evidence on suspects and covered up unlawful shootings by planting guns on people they shot. "Thumping" (beating up) suspects was routine, everyday behavior. Perez reported that suspects were interrogated and beaten while they were handcuffed. In one case a suspect was beaten until he vomited blood. In another case police officers raped a woman while they were on duty.

Perez has admitted that he and his partner shot Javier Francisco Ovando, an unarmed, handcuffed nineteen-year-old Latino, paralyzing him from the waist down. After they shot him, they planted a rifle on him to cover up their shooting. They perjured themselves at the man's trial, and Ovando was sentenced to twenty-three years in prison by a judge who chastised him for attacking two police officer–heros. Ovando spent two years and eleven months in prison in a wheelchair before Perez's testimony freed him. Although out of prison, he may never walk again. He is suing Los Angeles County for millions of dollars.

Perez testified that he helped cover up two other unjustified shootings. Juan Saldana was unarmed when he was shot by police officers. They planted a gun beside him and watched him bleed to death while they discussed with their supervisor how to get their story straight. In another instance police fired into a group celebrating New Year's Eve and shot two men. The police claimed that the two men had shot at police.

Forty criminal convictions have been reversed because of revelations of tainted evidence. Public defenders in Los Angeles predict that over 4,000 cases could be affected. So far twenty police officers have been suspended.

Police officers used their power for personal gain and as a weapon against people they did not like. They had witnesses to police malfeasance deported. A police officer whose tires had been slashed found the person he thought slashed his tires and left him naked in the middle of a rival gang's territory. Police officers routinely carried an extra gun with them to have as a plant if they shot an unarmed suspect. The exposure of crimes by the Rampart's unit has opened a can of worms, and other police units have been exposed as employing the same tactics.

As a result of the crimes of LAPD officers, several defendants pleaded guilty to crimes they did not commit. Under threat of longer prison sentences if they went to trial, they chose to admit guilt rather than take the chance. Joseph Jones was offered one such deal by the prosecutor: He could plead guilty to selling drugs and serve eight years in prison, or he could risk being convicted at trial as a three-time felon and be sentenced to life. He pleaded guilty and took the eight-year sentence even though the evidence was planted on him and police officers lied at his trial. Miguel Hernandez was given the option of sixteen months in prison if he pleaded guilty to possessing a weapon he had never had, or he could face a trial. If he were found guilty at the trial, he would be sentenced to at least four years. Because he had a prior record and was a Latino facing the accusations of a police officer, he said he believed he would be found guilty even though he was innocent. He accepted the plea bargain offered by the prosecutor.[3]

The Los Angeles Police Department has a history of corruption and brutality against minorities. On March 2, 1991, at around midnight, the LAPD stopped a black motorist, Rodney King, after a high-speed chase. As King got out of his car, the police knocked him to the ground and began beating him with their batons. An amateur video, later broadcast on television worldwide, revealed that King had been impaled by darts from an electronic TASER gun, repeatedly beaten with two-foot metal clubs, and violently kicked by police officers, all of whom were white. Before the episode ended, some twenty police officers arrived at the scene. No one tried to stop the beating. These events would have remained buried in the closed world of policing were it not for the fact that an amateur photographer saw what was happening from his porch and videotaped the incident. After the video was made public, four of the officers were brought to trial. The nearly all-white jury found the officers not guilty. To many people in the African American and Latino communities this was just another example of police brutality and discrimination that they witness every day. The acquittal of the four police officers was further proof that the standards of justice were different for whites and nonwhites. The verdict sparked one of the most violent and costly urban riots in U.S. history. Hundreds of people were injured, stores looted, and buildings burned, resulting in more than $1 billion in damage.

New York City also has a checkered history of dealing with minorities in the criminal justice system. White police officers in New York arrested Abner Louima, a Black Haitian immigrant. At the police station one of the officers, Justin Volpe, sodomized Louima by ramming the handle of a toilet plunger up Louima's rectum and forcing it into his mouth. Louima's bladder and colon were punctured, and he had several broken teeth. He spent two months in the hospital undergoing three operations.

After the attack, officer Volpe went around the precinct waving the dirty plunger and bragging about what he had done. One other police officer, Charles Schwarz, held Louima down, and two other officers witnessed the attack without trying to stop it.

The case received widespread publicity, partly due to the fact that Johnnie Cochran, who sucessfully defended O.J. Simpson, sued the New York Police on Louima's behalf. Officers Volpe and Schwarz were charged with assault. Volpe pleaded guilty; Schwarz tried to deny the charges and convinced the two officers who witnessed the attack to testify that Schwarz was not in the precinct when the attack occurred. Further investigation revealed that

Schwarz not only was in the precinct but that he held Louima down during the attack. Schwarz was also found guilty in the attack, and the two officers who falsely testified that he was not in the precinct were charged not only with failing to stop the attack but also with perjury and lying under oath about what transpired and who took part in the attack.

Examples of unwarranted police killings, brutality, and corruption are not isolated to New York and Los Angeles. In Oregon, police shot a man holding a cellular phone. They claimed they thought it was a gun. In a small California town several police officers shot and killed a woman sleeping in her car. Sixteen Washington, D.C., police officers were convicted of crimes in a fifteen-month period during 1999–2000. One was found guilty of two separate sexual assaults, one against a fourteen-year-old girl. A Washington, D.C., police officer testified before the city council that high-ranking police officers knew about corruption and police cover-ups but did nothing about it. A federal civil jury in Prince Georges County, Maryland, ordered the county to pay $4.1 million to Freddie McCollum Jr. for injuries suffered when he was arrested by the police and beaten. This same police department lost a civil suit costing taxpayers $647,000 for handcuffing a man to a post and leaving him there in the middle of the night. Prosecutors dropped charges against seven police officers for beating another black man, Elmer Clayton Newman Jr., whose death the state medical examiner ruled a homicide caused by cocaine use and injuries inflicted by the police. The charges were dropped because the officers "would not cooperate."[4]

Incidences of unwarranted shootings, brutality, and the use of excessive force have plagued Philadelphia's police department for years. In the 1970s, when former police commissioner Frank Rizzo was elected mayor, he promised to "make Atila the Hun look like a faggot. . . . The way to treat criminals is *spacco il capa* (bust their heads)." The U.S. Department of Justice found that during this period Philadelphia police were "37 times more likely to shoot unarmed citizens fleeing the site of non-violent crimes" than were police in New York City.[5]

In 1991 a black man in Philadelphia, Arthur Colbert, asked police for directions. Instead of giving him directions, the police arrested him on suspicion. The officers making the arrest, "Blondie" and Tommy Ryan, claimed he resembled a known drug dealer. He was taken to a run-down building in the neighborhood and beaten and threatened with death if he didn't admit to being "Hakim," the alleged drug dealer. He refused to lie about his identity, and after six hours of physical abuse he was released. Colbert got lucky. A police officer on duty the next day believed he was telling the truth when he related the sordid affair of the preceding night, and an extensive investigation ensued. When the photos of the two police officers who assaulted Colbert appeared in the newspaper, the department of internal investigations was flooded with complaints about police brutality and the planting of evidence on suspects. The two officers who beat Colbert and three other policemen were tried and sentenced (one received a ten-month jail sentence; four others were sentenced to prison). The investigation implicated fifty other police officers and a host of crimes, including stealing money confiscated from drug busts, perjury in testifying in court, planting evidence, and rampant police violence against suspects.

As Blondie explained to a reporter, "The pressure is to produce, to show activity, to get the collars [i.e., arrests]. It's all about numbers, like the body count in Vietnam. The rest of the system determines if you got the right guy or not." Unfortunately, the "rest of the system" does not determine if "you got the right guy or not."[6]

In Irvington, New Jersey, Max Antoine, a paralegal, was awakened at 2 A.M. when police forcefully entered his house without a warrant and began searching it. They had been tipped off that there were drugs there. Max questioned the right of the police to tear up the house, for which the police beat him with a nightstick, kicked him, shoved his head through a glass door, sprayed him with a chemical irritant, put him in jail for two days, and denied him medical attention. He was so severely beaten that he suffered bowel and bladder damage, a broken jaw, spinal injuries, and a fractured eye socket.[7] No drugs were found.

Every objective investigation of police misuse of force and police brutality conducted in the United States since the 1930s has come to the same conclusion as a recent study of fourteen U.S. cities by Human Rights Watch:

> Police brutality is one of the most serious, enduring, and divisive human rights violations in the United States. The problem is nationwide, and its nature is institutionalized. . . . Police officers engage in unjustified shootings, severe beatings, fatal choking, and unnecessar-

> ily rough physical treatment in cities throughout the United States, while their police superiors, city officials, and the Justice Department fail to act decisively to restrain or penalize such acts or even to record the full magnitude of the problem.[8]

The conclusions of Human Rights Watch echo the findings of the 1931 Wickerhsam Commission. The commission, made up of representatives of the Northeast white establishment, expressed grave concern and shock at the extent of police brutality and corruption it found in its investigation. At the time, the use of physical force to coerce confessions from suspects was standard procedure. It took an unusually heinous example, the case of *Brown v. Mississippi,* for the U.S. Supreme Court to rule that confessions were inadmissible unless they were "voluntary." The open use of force by police to coerce confessions declined, but the use of police brutality only went underground and became more sophisticated: Ways of brutalizing suspects, such as cutting off air by choking without leaving any marks, became part of the unofficial police manual passed down, like folk knowledge, from one generation of police officers to the next.[9]

The culture of policing encourages police violence by adopting a military model in police training and a military structure of organization. As a Philadelphia police officer now serving time in prison observed about his fourteen weeks at the police academy, "It was mostly firearms training first aid and war stories. They taught a bit about things like probable cause—just to say they had taught it—but the message was clear: What you really do as a cop you learn on the street from the veterans, and you could be sure, as they said, that it was nothing like what you learned at the academy."[10]

The use of violence by the police is seen as necessary and is rewarded formally and informally. Even when citizen complaints succeed in exposing violence and a victim is awarded large sums of money by the courts, the officers responsible are not held accountable. In the culture of the police, the Dirty Harrys are revered just as they are transformed into heroic figures in the media.

Because not all law enforcement agents support the misuse of force, one might think using unnecessary violence would be risky business, for an offending officer could be reported. Even more strongly held than the value of being macho is the inviolate code of silence when it comes to reporting crimes by fellow officers. Anyone who reports another police officer for *anything* is branded a snitch. Allegiance to the force above all other values provides an arena in which individual police officers are free to enforce the law however they see fit. Given the siege mentality of police officers and police departments, it is inevitable that some will step over the line and impose their own brand of law and order on those they see as deserving punishment.

Police Corruption

Between 1994 and 1997, 508 law enforcement officers were convicted of corruption. Over twice that many officers were convicted of crimes of theft, burglary, organized crime, and dealing drugs. In 1997 and 1998 law enforcement officers in New York, New Jersey, Starr County, Texas, Detroit, and Cleveland were arrested. In Cleveland alone fifty-nine law enforcement officers were arrested and charged with police corruption.[11]

Here are just a few of the many recent examples of police corruption:

- In Washington, D.C., in January 2000 a veteran policeman was charged with trafficking in cocaine for the entire nine years he was on the force.
- Three Detroit police officers were charged on January 14, 1998, with conspiring to commit a robbery of approximately $1 million.
- The sheriff, a justice of the peace, and five county jailers in Starr County, Texas, were charged with bribery.
- Nine New York and New Jersey police officers were charged with racketeering involving the protection of prostitution and illegal gambling.

The structure of policing invites widespread corruption. The principal source of the corruption is the billions of dollars a year in profits generated by the underground economy in drugs, gambling, loan-sharking, money-laundering, and prostitution. In my research on organized crime in Seattle, I discovered a symbiotic relationship between organized crime and the police that made it impossible to differentiate between them. Police officers from street patrolmen to police chiefs as well as members of the prosecuting attorney's office not only accepted payoffs from people who organized illegal gambling, prostitution, and drug sales; in fact the police and prosecutors were instrumental in organizing and managing these activities.[12] Seattle is not an exception—it is the rule.

In 1993 the Mollen Commission in New York sat stonefaced as police officers told how they had accepted bribes from drug dealers, engaged in trafficking drugs, and stole drugs to sell them. Fourteen New York police officers were charged and eleven others were disciplined for complicity in drug-trafficking. Indeed, one can scarcely keep up with the corruption of police officers in the United States: A recent sting operation by the FBI netted twelve Washington, D.C., police officers who were selling drugs themselves and taking payoffs from drug dealers in their precincts.[13] In all, seventy-seven police officers in Washington faced criminal charges. Only weeks before the arrest of the twelve police officers, twelve corrections officers were arrested on charges of taking drugs into Lorton, the District of Columbia prison, and selling them to inmates.

Former police chiefs in Rochester, New York, and Detroit have been convicted of drug-related offenses, and police officers in Philadelphia, Miami, Los Angeles, and Cleveland have been convicted of accepting bribes, theft, and complicity in drug-trafficking in recent years.[14] In 1997 the FBI brought charges of corruption and accepting bribes against fifty police officers in Cleveland, and more than 300 police officers nationwide were indicted between 1996 and 1998.

Some police corruption reflects the fact that in order to be an effective undercover agent the police officer must become a drug user. People selling drugs are not going to provide drugs on a regular basis to an agent who himself or herself is never seen consuming the drugs. In this way the government is in effect forcing agents to become drug users in order to do their job. Some of these agents then steal drugs to support the habit they developed while fulfilling their assignment as an undercover officer. Others accept bribes and steal drugs simply for profit.

It is not only the officers in the streets who give in to the temptation to profit from the illegal business in drugs. In Louisiana, for the first time in the 200-year history of the federal judiciary, a federal district judge was convicted of taking a $100,000 bribe from a drug smuggler.[15] An online search of newspaper articles on NEXIS (which represent only a fraction of the total cases) revealed the following list of cases in recent years:

In December 1999 an undercover FBI agent who infiltrated a Boston organized crime network was indicted by a federal grand jury on five counts of racketeering, conspiracy, and obstruction of justice. He pleaded not guilty.

A lawyer and two former judges were found guilty in San Diego of corrupting the San Diego Superior Court by engaging in a scheme in which the lawyer gave the judges gifts and cash in exchange for favored treatment of his lawsuits.

Since 1983, at least fifteen DEA agents have been convicted of federal felonies.

May 1989: Two veteran DEA agents, Drew Bunnel and Al Iglesias, were charged with taking bribes from a drug dealer.

April 1989: DEA agent Jorge Villar was indicted for selling confidential information and names of drug informants to drug dealers. When arrested, he was carrying a briefcase with $350,000 in bank certificates of deposit.

July 1990: A sheriff's deputy in Clark County, Washington, Herbert Pacheco, was convicted of conspiracy to commit murder, conspiracy to deliver cocaine, and attempted cocaine delivery.

March 1988: Four New York City police officers were convicted of the beating and torture of a drug dealer.

October 1988: Tommy Pruitt, head of a Georgia drug task force, was sentenced to fifteen years in prison for selling drugs valuing at least $10,000 to a drug dealer.

July 1990: Carlos Simon, a Hialeah, Florida, police officer, was sentenced to thirty years for the murders of an alleged drug dealer and his girlfriend.

March 1993: Edward K. O'Brien, a former DEA agent, was sentenced to six years in prison for cocaine smuggling and embezzlement of $140,000 in drug money.

October 1990: Eddie Hill, DEA supervisor, went on trial for embezzling drug money and filing false vouchers.

June 1990: the police chief of Brockton, Massachusetts, received a seven- to ten-year year sentence for stealing cocaine from the police department's evidence room. Three hundred seventy five cases had to be dismissed because of the missing evidence.

January 1990: Four Philadelphia police officers who were members of a special antidrug unit were sentenced to prison for stealing money and drugs from the drug dealers they arrested.

In 1994 the DEA agent who arrested Manuel Noreiga in Panama diverted $700,000 in laundered drug profits into his own bank account in Switzerland.

In 1998 an INS officer in Miami was part of a Haitian gang that smuggled thirty-three tons of cocaine into the United States.[16]

The list could be expanded indefinitely. Suffice it to say that the corruption of law enforcement agents is ubiquitous at all levels of policing—municipal, state, and federal—in the United States.[17]

The Corruption of Due Process of Law

In Chapter 4 we demonstrated how bribing witnesses to testify against defendants corrupted the due process of law.

Law enforcement officers and prosecutors want to get convictions. They may want to further their careers, or they may want to see someone they "know" is guilty be convicted even if they do not have sufficient evidence to convince a judge or jury. In either case, the need for convictions incites agents to plant evidence, to doctor evidence, and to lie at trials. In March 1993 seven Los Angeles County Sheriff Department narcotics agents were found guilty of planting cocaine in the bag of a suspected dealer. In Oakland drug agents were found guilty of planting drugs, beating suspects, and sexually assaulting them. A Los Angeles County Sheriff Department officer planted heroin on a woman to whom he owed money. Again, these are but a smattering of the cases: The practice of illegally planting drugs on suspects or in their homes is rampant and for the most part goes undetected.

According to an investigation by the inspector general, FBI agents from the forensic laboratory distorted testimony at the O.J. Simpson trial and altered evidence at the laboratory. True to form, only two of the dozen or more agents responsible for these crimes were sanctioned—with a letter of reprimand.[18] Again the culture of protecting one's own took precedence over seeking answers as to why such things go on.

Local and federal law enforcement agencies today have an even greater incentive to violate the law in pursuit of criminal convictions than in the past. The property of suspected felons, including people in possession of small amounts of drugs, can be confiscated, and a portion of the value of the property is turned over to the law enforcement agency. Local and federal law enforcement agencies, including the DEA and the FBI, have benefited immensely from the houses, boats, airplanes, and expensive automobiles confiscated as a result of arrests of drug dealers. The opportunity for abuse is apparently too tempting to resist. Cheryl Sanders of Long Beach, California, was stopped for speeding in Sulphur, Louisiana, by three police officers. Instead of giving her a ticket, they handcuffed her and took her to jail, where she was forced to disrobe and was searched. No drugs or other illegal items were found on her or in her car. The police informed her, however, that although she was not being charged with anything other than speeding, they were going to confiscate her car. Louisiana's 1995 civil asset forfeiture law allows police to seize vehicles if there is "suspicion" that the owner of the vehicle is a drug dealer. It took Sanders seven months and a large legal bill to force the police to return her car.

The U.S. government uses asset forfeiture laws indiscriminately and often without adequate protection for the accused. In one case three men unloaded cocaine onto the property of a deceased homeowner. Because the government claimed the owner had known one of the men (in testimony, the defendant who knew the owner was vague and claimed only to have met "someone named George," the homeowner's first name), DEA agents confiscated the house. U.S. District Judge James Paine ordered the government to return the ownership of the house to the owner's heirs and chastised the officers who seized the property for providing "no credible evidence" that the owner of the house had anything to do with drug-trafficking.[19]

The Political Smoke Screen

It is not only law enforcement agencies that hide behind the smoke screen of crime in the streets. Politicians can deflect other issues and avoid responsibility by fanning the flames of fear about crime.

It is ironic that two of the highest-ranking politicians in U.S. history exposed for systematic criminality while in office ran for election on a platform of law and order. Vice President Spiro Agnew was convicted of accepting bribes and payoffs, and President Richard Nixon was forced to resign or be impeached for a host of crimes including conspiracy to commit burglary and obstructing justice.

The latest president to use fear of crime to gain political advantage, Bill Clinton, also has lived under a cloud of allegations of corruption, payoffs, and obstructing justice. As Martin Gross says in *The Political Racket*, "Corruption is rife in America, from the smallest communities to the West Wing of the White House, whichever party occupies it."

Even though a very small proportion of law enforcement effort is devoted to ferreting out corruption in politics, the FBI nonetheless stumbles upon it whenever it takes the time to look. Local law enforcement agencies, themselves embedded in corruption, simply turn a blind eye. Even though there is minimal surveillance, the best lawyers money can buy, and political clout to protect the corrupt, political corruption is exposed with alarming regularity. In 1995 the FBI brought over 520 indictments of 700 individuals on charges of political corruption. In 1996, 470 cases charged 643 individuals, and in 1997 there were 487 cases charging 643 individuals. The conviction rate in these cases is over 80 percent. In 1997 alone over $30 million in fines was collected.[20]

Since 1970 thirty members of Congress have been *convicted* (and many more accused) of accepting bribes, racketeering, perjury, padding payrolls with relatives and friends who pay them kickbacks, mail fraud, sex with minors, and tax evasion. In the House of Representatives, Joshua Eilberg, Charles Diggs, Frederick Richmond, Daniel Flood, George Hansen, Mario Biaggi, Patrick Swindall, Alberg Bustamente, and Dan Rostenkowski are but a few of the infamous congressmen convicted of serious crimes.

In 1993, 2,733 elected and appointed public officials were convicted, indicted, or were awaiting trial for crimes of bribery, fraud, extortion, and conflict of interest. These cases are but the tip of the proverbial iceberg.

As mentioned, Spiro Agnew was forced to resign the vice presidency when a grand jury began investigating allegations that he received a $50,000 payment to secure government contracts and had received $1,000 a week from contractors, architects, and builders while serving as governor of Maryland. Agnew told the court that bribes for politicians were so necessary a part of doing business in the state that companies built it into their annual budget.Martin L. Gross, *The Political Racket* (New York: Ballantine Books, 1996).

The billions of dollars in campaign contributions that flow into the coffers of politicians are the most blatant and the most commonplace bribes in politics. They, by design, succeed in buying legislation, political influence, appointments to public offices, and contacts. Lobbyists pay between $10,000 and $100,000 to attend dinners with high-ranking politicians, including the president and the most powerful members of Congress. These dinners raise upward of $15 million in one evening for political campaigns.

It is no surprise that when Bill Gates of Microsoft was under investigation for monopolistic practices in 1997 his contributions to the political parties soared in 1998. A few days after a judge found Microsoft liable for antitrust violations, Gates was a guest at the White House, where he posed for a photo-op with President Clinton and the president of the World Bank. The tobacco industry vastly increased its political campaign contributions when it was threatened with the passage of laws that would raise cigarette taxes and force them to pay billions of dollars in compensation for the health costs incurred due to smoking. The payoffs of the tobacco industry were partially successful: The laws were defeated. When its workers went on strike UPS, which has for years been among the heaviest contributors to Republican campaigns, increased its contributions even further and added Democratic politicians to its list of donors.

If the consequences were not so dire, the sanctimonious statements by large contributors to political campaigns—that they are giving out of the spirit of democracy or because it gives them personal pleasure—would be amusing. Corporations and individuals that give lavishly to political campaigns and subsequently receive government favors worth ten times their contributions deny any connection as surely as the tobacco industry for years lied about the known connection between cigarette smoking and cancer. Bernard L. Schwartz, CEO of Loral Corporation, donated over $1 million to the Democratic Party. After his initial donation of $100,000, he requested that he be included on a trade mission to China. He was given a seat on the mission, and a meeting was arranged between Schwartz and a Chinese communications minister that, according to Schwartz, "helped open doors that were not open before." The doors it opened led to a decision by President Clinton, against the advice of the Justice Department, to allow Schwartz's company to launch a commercial telecommunications satellite aboard a Chinese rocket. Schwartz insists that his contributions to the Democrats have nothing to do with these favorable decisions. Schwartz says he contributes "purely for the enjoyment of giving."

There is no difference between these vast political campaign contributions and bribery. Indeed, those responsible for getting the contributions often engage in what on the streets would be called a "shakedown." When representatives of dairy-farmer organizations sought to raise the price they could charge for milk by having the federal milk price supports increased, then–Treasury Secretary John B. Connally told President Nixon that he was "going to tell them they've got to put so much money directly at your disposal."[21]

In the 1998 congressional campaign the Business-Industry Political Action Committee (BIPAC) threatened to shift its support from the Republicans to the Democrats unless it was given assurance that the Republicans would pass legislation favored by BIPAC. The threat worked: The legislation was promised, and campaign contributions were reinstated.[22]

State-Organized Crime

Crime in the streets also obscures the prevalence of state-organized crime, that is, criminal acts committed by government officials in the course of their duties. The complicity of the CIA in the smuggling of illegal drugs, particularly cocaine and heroin, has become part of the government's unofficial policy since at least the Vietnam War and is a prime example of state-organized crime.

The CIA and Drugs

CIA agents have supported international trafficking in heroin and cocaine by transporting opium and heroin on airlines owned by the CIA, obtaining freedom from prosecution of known drug traffickers who were informants or operatives of the CIA, and cooperating with heroin and cocaine traffickers in return for their support of CIA operations in Southeast Asia, Latin America, Pakistan, and Afghanistan.

At the height of the Cold War the CIA virtually established Burma, Laos, and Thailand in Southeast Asia (the so-called Golden Triangle) as the world's leading supplier of opium and heroin, replacing the monopoly formerly enjoyed by Turkey and other Middle East countries.[23]

The CIA in Vietnam

The U.S. military and the CIA did not invent complicity with opium smugglers in Southeast Asia; they inherited the practice from the French who, from the early days of colonialism in Indochina, depended on the profits from opium to support the colonial government. When the communist insurgency in Vietnam began to gain momentum, aiding the opium-producing Hill tribes was a central ingredient in gaining their support. In addition, the profits from the opium trade were used to finance the war against the communists.

Because of the Hill tribes' proximity to the Chinese border, both France and the United States depended on the military support of such tribes in Burma, Cambodia, Laos, Thailand, and Vietnam. That support, in turn, required that the French and U.S. intelligence services cooperate with the production and distributions of the tribes' only cash crop: opium. Air America, the CIA airline in Vietnam, regularly transported bundles of opium from airstrips in Laos, Cambodia, and Burma to Saigon and Hong Kong.

An American soldier stationed at Long Cheng, the secret CIA military base in northern Laos during the Vietnam War, observed:

> So long as the Meo leadership could keep their wards in the boondocks fighting and dying in the name of, for these unfortunates any-

way, some nebulous cause . . . the Meo leadership [was paid off] in the form of a carte-blanch to exploit U.S.-supplied airplanes and communication gear to the end of greatly streamlining the opium operations.[24]

Laotian Army General Ouane Rattikone told me in an interview in 1974 that he was the principal overseer of the shipment of opium out of the Golden Triangle via Air America. At the CIA base in Long Cheng were a number of military officers whose careers in state-organized crime continued after Vietnam: General Richard Secord, Thomas Clines, Theodore Schackley, and Michael Hand.[25]

U.S. law did not permit the CIA or any of its agents to engage in the smuggling of opium. The CIA officially denied involvement even in the face of overwhelming evidence to the contrary. Thus the United States was implicated in the perpetuation of a form of state-organized crime that, ironically, was responsible for the addiction and death of its own soldiers and subsequently for a dramatic increase in heroin addiction in the United States.[26]

Supporting the Contras

As in Vietnam, in order to support the contras in their war against the leftist Nicaraguan government, the CIA and other government agencies knowingly cooperated with cocaine and marihuana smugglers in Latin America.[27]

In 1986 the government admitted in testimony before Congress that Adolfo Chamorro's contra group, which was supported by the CIA, was helping a Columbian drug trafficker transport drugs into the United States. Adolfo Chamorro was arrested in April 1986 for his involvement. The CIA-owned airline, Southern Air Transport, was a key link in the illegal transfer of arms to the contras (see discussion below) and the shipment of marijuana and cocaine from Latin America to the United States. Independent counsel Lawrence E. Walsh was given a report detailing a connection between a Columbian cocaine trafficker and Southern Air Transport.[28] A Southern Air Transport pilot, Mike Toliver, testified that he met twice with Rafeal Quintero and returned to the United States with 25,000 pounds of marijuana.[29]

- In January 1983 two contra leaders in Costa Rica persuaded the Justice Department to return over $36,000 in drug profits to dealer Julio Zavala and Carlos Cabezas to aid the Contras.[30]
- Michael Palmer, a drug king in Miami, testified that the U.S. State Department's Nicaraguan Humanitarian Assistance office contracted with his company, Vortex Sales and Leasing, to take humanitarian aid to the contras despite knowledge that he was a major drug trafficker. Because of his State Department contract, Palmer claims that he was able to smuggle $40 million in marijuana to the United States from 1977 to 1985.[31]

The Afghan War

Alexander Cockburn and Jeffrey St. Clair, in their excellent account of CIA and other government agencies' complicity in drug-trafficking point out that U.S. support of the mujahideen in Pakistan and Afghanistan once again contributed to a substantial increase in the production of opium and heroin. Gulbuddin Hekmatyar was a leading member of the mujahideen and one of the leading heroin producers in the Middle East; Cockburn and St. Clair describe the CIA connection:

> Using the weapons [provided by the CIA] to get control of the opium fields Hekmatyar and his men would urge the peasants, at gun point, to increase production [of opium]. They would collect the raw opium and bring it back to Hekmatyar's six heroin factories in the town of Koh-i-Soltan. One of Hekmatyar's chief rivals in the mujahideen, Mullah Nassim, controlled the opium poppy fields in the Helmand Valley, producing 260 tons of opium a year. His brother, Mohammed Rasul, defended this agricultural enterprise by stating: "We must grow and sell opium to fight our holy war against the Russian non-believers."[32]

The rationalization offered by Rasul runs throughout the history of U.S. complicity in crime, from support of the Italian Mafia after World War II, to assassination plots forged between government agencies and organized crime figures, to support of international narcotics smuggling in Southeast Asia, Latin America, Afghanistan, and Pakistan.

Arms Smuggling

The illegal smuggling of arms became as important as the smuggling of cocaine and marijuana during the war in Nicaragua. To a significant extent, U.S. involvement in narcotics after the Vietnam War must be understood as a means of funding the purchase of military weapons for nations and insurgent groups that cannot be funded legally through congressional allocations or where U.S. law prohibits support.

In violation of U.S. law, members of the National Security Council, the Department of Defense, and the Central Intelligence Agency carried out a plan to sell millions of dollars' worth of arms to Iran and use profits from these sales to illegally support the contras in Nicaragua.[33] The Boland Amendment, effective in 1985, prohibited any U.S. official from directly or indirectly assisting the contras. Cut off from any legal avenues of support, then–CIA Director William Casey contacted Lieutenant Colonel Oliver North of the National Security Council. Casey instructed him to set up a self-sustaining enterprise that would be held accountable to only a few people. An article in *The Guardian* discusses the "secret team" of U.S. operatives in Central America. Theodore Shackley allegedly led this team, and its members included General Richard Secord, General Singlaub, Tom Clines, and other veterans of the 1961 invasion of Cuba.[34]

Senator Daniel Inouye of Hawaii claimed that this "secret government within our government" waging war in Third World countries was part of President Ronald Reagan's doctrine.[35] Weapons were sold to Iran contrary to the administration's official policy and the Illegal Arms Export Control Act, which made the sale of unlicensed arms to Iran unlawful. The CIA through the Pentagon obtained the weapons. On four different occasions in 1986, Secretary of Defense Caspar Weinberger ordered the transfer of weapons from U.S. Army stocks to the CIA without the knowledge of Congress.[36] The arms were then transferred to middlemen such as Iranian arms dealer Yaacov Nimrodi, exiled Iranian arms dealer

Manucher Ghorbanifar, and Saudi Arabian businessman Adman Khashoggi. Weapons were also flown directly to the contras, and funds from the sale of weapons were diverted to financially support contra warfare.[37]

Assassinations and Murder

The assassination of political leaders whose programs run counter to the interests of a nation has become almost commonplace in international politics. It is one of the most sinister of modern-day state-organized crimes.

It is well established that the French intelligence agency hired a man named Christian David (who also had connections with Robert Vesco and the U.S. Drug Enforcement Agency) to assassinate Moroccan leftist leader Ben Barka.[38] Agents of the CIA and other government officials have planned the assassination of dozens of foreign leaders, including President Ngo Dinh Diem in Vietnam, Patrice Lumumba in the Congo, and Rafael Trujillo in the Dominican Republic.[39] All three were assassinated; whether the acts were carried out by U.S. agents or others, we will never know.

It is a crime to conspire to commit murder, including the assassination of foreign leaders, but no one ever was charged, and no one ever will be. Whether the assassinations of Trujillo, Diem, and Lumumba were the result of U.S. government plots will never be known, but assassination attempts on Cuban leader Fidel Castro can be unequivocally laid at the door of the U.S. government. Testimony before the U.S. Congress revealed that the CIA engaged the services of organized crime figures, including Chicago's Sam Giancana, California's John Roselli, and Florida's Santo Trafficante Jr., in a plot to assassinate Fidel Castro.[40] (See Table 7.1.)

On May 8, 1985, a car bomb exploded in Beirut, killing over eighty people. A Lebanese counterterrorist unit working with the CIA set the bomb. Senator Daniel Patrick Moynihan said when he was chair of the Senate Intelligence Committee, President Reagan ordered the CIA to form a small antiterrorist effort in the Mideast. Two sources testified that the CIA was working with the group that planted the bomb to kill the Shiite leader Hussein Fadlallah.[41]

Contra leader Eden Pastora was speaking at a press conference in La Penca on October 30, 1984, when a bomb exploded, injuring seventeen, including Pastora, and killing eight people attending

TABLE 7.1 Assassination Conspiracies and Attempts by the U.S. Government

The U.S. bombing of Iraq, on June 26, 1993, in retaliation for an alleged Iraqi plot to assassinate former president George Bush, "was essential," said President Clinton, "to send a message to those who engage in state-sponsored terrorism ... and to affirm the expectation of civilized behavior among nations."

Following is a list of prominent foreign individuals whose assassination (or planning for same) the United States has been involved in since the end of World War II. The list does not include several assassinations in various parts of the world carried out by anti-Castro Cubans employed by the CIA and headquartered in the United States.

Year	*Planned Victim*
1949	Kim Koo, Korean opposition leader
1950s	CIA/Neo-Nazi hit list of numerous political figures in West Germany
1955	José Antonio Remon, President of Panama
1950s	Chou En-lai, Prime minister of China, several attempts on his life
1950s	Sukarno, President of Indonesia
1951	Kim Il Sung, Premier of North Korea
1950s (mid)	Claro M. Recto, Philippines opposition leader
1955	Jawaharlal Nehru, Prime Minister of India
1957	Gamal Abdul Nasser, President of Egypt
1959 and 1963	Norodom Sihanouk, leader of Cambodia
1960	Brig. Gen. Abdul Karim Kassem, leader of Iraq
1950s–70s	José Figueres, President of Costa Rica, two attempts on his life
1961	François "Papa Doc" Duvalier, leader of Haiti
1961	Patrice Lumumba, Prime Minister of the Congo (Zaire)
1961	Gen. Rafael Trujillo, leader of Dominican Republic
1963	Ngo Dinh Diem, President of South Vietnam
1960s	Fidel Castro, President of Cuba, many attempts on his life
1960s	Raúl Castro, high official in government of Cuba
1965	Francisco Caamaño, Dominican Republic opposition leader
1965	Pierre Ngendandumwe, Prime Minister of Burundi
1965–1966	Charles de Gaulle, President of France
1967	Che Guevara, Cuban leader
1970	Salvador Allende, President of Chile
1970	Gen. Rene Schneider, Commander-in-Chief of Army, Chile
1970s, 1981	General Omar Torrijos, leader of Panama
1972	General Manuel Noriega, Chief of Panama Intelligence
1975	Mobutu Sese Seko, President of Zaire
1976	Michael Manley, Prime Minister of Jamaica
1980–1986	Muammar Qaddafi, leader of Libya, several plots and attempts upon his life.
1982	Ayatollah Khomeini, leader of Iran
1983	Gen. Ahmed Dlimi, Moroccan Army commander
1983	Miguel d'Escoto, Foreign Minister of Nicaragua
1984	The nine *comandantes* of the Sandinista National Directorate
1985	Sheikh Mohammed Hussein Fadlallah, Lebanese Shiite leader (80 people killed in the attempt)
1991	Saddam Hussein, leader of Iraq

SOURCE: William Blum, *Killing Hope* (Monroe, Maine: Common Courage Press), 453.

the press conference. Pastora was at odds with the CIA, who wanted him to unite with the Nicaraguan Democratic Force. There is some evidence that Per Anker Hansen set off the bomb when he posed as a reporter under orders from Theodore Shackley, Thomas Clines, General Secord, General Singlaub, and Ed Wilson.[42] There is stronger evidence to support the conflicting theory that John Hull, Robert Owen, Felipe Vidal, and Adolfo Calero merged their operations and hired Amac Galil to assassinate Pastora.[43] In either case, CIA operatives are implicated in the murder of eight people and the maiming of seventeen others.

Assassination plots have been planned by the DEA in an attempt to control international drug-smuggling.[44] Faced with the difficult task of prosecuting major financiers, many of whom were high-level officials of foreign governments, intelligence agents, and industrialists, the DEA conspired to commit murder. Lou Conein, also known as "Black Luigi," left a position in the White House in 1972 to organize a Special Operations Group within the DEA. He brought with him twelve CIA paramilitary specialists on loan to the DEA. George Crile, writing in the *Washington Post* on June 13, 1976, quotes a DEA official: "When you get down to it, Conein was organizing an assassination program. He was frustrated by the big-time operators who were just too insulated to get to. . . . Meetings were held to decide whom to target and what method of assassination to employ."

In 1978 the investigative journalist Jim Hougan wrote:

> My own sources tend to confirm Crile's. The scenario they describe is one which some members of the "Dirty Dozen" [the CIA para-militarists assigned to Conein and the DEA] would assist their boss in selecting targets for assassination. Once those targets were approved, booby traps obtained for The Company [the CIA] would be issued and—there is no other word—contracts put out.[45]

The actual assassination was to be carried out by hired killers, usually citizens of the country of the targeted victim. The hired assassins were to be provided with advice and the necessary antipersonnel devices. According to an affidavit filed in a Miami court: Theodore Shackley, Thomas Clines, and Richard Armitage (a U.S. Navy officer who later became assistant secretary of state for international security affairs), "In the early 1970s . . . set up their own private anti-communism assassination program in Southeast Asia.

The operations later continued in the Middle East, in support of Shah Mohammed Reza Pahlavi of Iran, and allegedly were funded with money from Laotian-based trading in opium."[46]

The official records, including testimony by participants in these conspiracies before the U.S. Congress and in court, make it abundantly clear that the crime of conspiring to commit murder is not infrequent in the intelligence agencies and other offices of the U.S. government. Since many of the people who were the targets of these plans were murdered, one suspects that the crime may not have been merely a conspiracy.

Another criminal conspiracy in which the CIA admits participation is the publication of the manual *Psychological Operation in Guerrilla Warfare*, which was distributed to the people of Nicaragua and describes how they should proceed to commit murder, sabotage, vandalism, and violent acts in order to undermine the government. This act was prohibited by a Reagan executive order in 1981 that forbade any U.S. participation in foreign assassinations.[47] In clear violation of U.S. law, however, several CIA officials provided Iranians with tactical military advice and military intelligence information on Iraq.[48]

The CIA also trained and advised Chile's secret service prior to and after the election of President Salvador Allende in 1970. This CIA-trained secret service plotted the overthrow of Allende and the murder of General Renee Schneider and was responsible for Allende's suicide (or his murder, depending on which cause of his death one believes). Later, after General Augusto Pinochet became president of Chile, he vastly increased the powers of the secret service, which he called DINA. One of its first missions was Operation Condor. FBI Agent Robert Scherer sent a top-secret message to Washington in which he stated: "Operation Condor involves the formation of special teams from member countries to travel anywhere in the world to non-member countries to carry out sanctions including assassinations."[49] The Chilean government thereby institutionalized murder and terrorism as a mainstay of governance.

The CIA and the FBI also covered up murders committed by their informants, murders that may have been ordered by the CIA. A Cuban exile, Ricardo "Monkey" Morales, who immigrated to Miami in 1960, was employed by the CIA and the FBI. Although in the FBI's employ, Morales went to Venezuela, where he joined the Venezuelan secret police as head of security at Caracas International Airport. In court testimony and published interviews, Morales admits that he planted a bomb on an Air Cubana flight from Caracas that killed seventy-three passengers. He and the Miami police both testified in court that this was a CIA job and that he was acting under their instructions. He was unrepentant: "If I had to, I would do it over again."[50]

Morales was arrested in Miami overseeing the shipment of ten tons of marijuana. Because of his status as an undercover agent for the FBI and the CIA, he was never convicted. He openly admits to bombings, murder, and assassination attempts, yet he has never served a day in prison. In 1968, while he was a contract agent for the CIA, he admitted murdering a Cuban exile and tried to execute another. While employed by the FBI he murdered another Cuban exile, Eladio Ruiz, in broad daylight in downtown Miami. The execution was "reportedly carried out as a warning to Castro sympathizers."[51] Morales was never prosecuted for any of his crimes. His protection from prosecution for murder, terrorism, and drug-dealing ended only when he was shot and killed in a Miami bar in 1982.

President Reagan approved a plan for the CIA to "destabilize" the Libyan government of Colonel Muammar Qaddafi. This plot, the *Washington Post* reported, included an effort to "lure [Qaddafi] into some foreign adventure of terrorist exploit that would give a growing number of Qaddafi opponents in the Libyan military a chance to seize power, or such a foreign adventure might give one of Qaddafi's neighbors, such as Algeria or Egypt, a justification for responding to Qaddafi militarily." A CIA report argued that the United States should "stimulate" Qaddafi's fall by encouraging disaffected elements in the Libyan army who could be spurred to assassination attempts.[52]

Miscellaneous State-Organized Crimes

Law prohibits the CIA from conducting covert intelligence activities in the United States. To engage in such activities is a criminal offense against the person or persons who are the target of investigation. From 1960 to 1975 (and perhaps beyond), the CIA engaged in covert intelligence activities designed to reveal the political attitudes and activities of hundreds of American citizens.[53] The CIA carried out a letter-opening campaign against U.S. citizens without court approval and in violation of state and federal laws. This campaign lasted for at least twelve years.[54]

The CIA organized a group of prostitutes and provided them with lavishly decorated apartments to which they could bring clients. The clients were then given drugs, and their responses were recorded by CIA observers (including medical doctors) hidden behind one-way mirrors and paintings. The drugs were being tested to see if they would induce amnesia, render a subject suggestible, alter sexual patterns, induce aberrant behavior, get the subject to reveal information he otherwise would not, and create dependency in the subject. At least one of the subjects died as a result of the experience.[55] There is, needless to say, nothing in U.S. law that permits such behavior. The failure to prosecute the perpetrators of these crimes was rationalized on the grounds that the testimony of the prostitutes or their clients would not stand up in court.

The FBI and the CIA also engaged in criminal slander designed to disrupt, harass, and discredit legally constituted political parties and political movements in the United States. From 1960 to 1970 the FBI organized an illegal top-secret campaign (COINTELPRO) against civil rights and antiwar movements. COINTELPRO included planting false documents, threatening peoples' lives, breaking and entering private offices and homes, stealing documents, and illegal (i.e., criminal) surveillance. The extent of such programs in the United States may never be known, but revelations from documents secured under the Freedom of Information Act suggest widespread and long-term criminal activities of the state organized for the suppression of political parties and ideologies unpopular among government officials.[56]

The Reagan administration and the CIA engaged in prohibited covert activity to influence public opinion on Nicaraguan policy. The Office of Public Diplomacy for Nicaragua and El Salvador was formulated by Reagan in January 1983 and run by Oliver North and the National Security Council. The office contracted with International Business Communications beginning in 1984 to influence public opinion after Congress cut off aid to the contras. The General Accounting Office found in its investigation of these events that the CIA was guilty of "violating statutes, conducting unfair bidding practices, and the misappropriation of $263,000 between June of 1983 and February of 1986."[57]

Corporate Crime

Corporate crimes are more costly, dangerous, and violent than the robberies, burglaries, assaults, and murders so ceremoniously reported by the FBI in the Uniform Crime Reports. The Joint Economic Committee of the U.S. Congress estimates the yearly losses from street crimes at $4 billion. The Senate Judiciary Subcommittee on Antitrust and Monopoly, estimates the cost of corporate crime at over $200 billion a year—fifty times the cost of street crime. Even this may be a gross underestimate: The savings-and-loan collapse alone cost the taxpayers some $150–175 billion.[58] Accounting for interest that the government will pay on the increased debt it accrued as a result of the collapse, the total cost will exceed $500 billion.[59]

The costs of corporate crime in death and personal injury are even greater: "On September 3, 1991 an explosion and fire at the Imperial Food Products chicken processing plant in Hamlet, North Carolina, killed 25 workers and injured another 56. . . . Fire doors that would have led the workers to safety were deliberately kept locked 'to keep employees from stealing chicken nuggets.'"[60] A government report estimates yearly deaths from industrially caused diseases and accidents at 100,000 a year. Since up to 50 percent of industrial accidents may be caused by the violation of factory safety and health regulations, the death toll directly resulting from crimes by corporations is substantial.

Yet most corporate crimes receive barely a mention in the press, except in the business section of newspapers. Compared to the amount of money and personnel spent annually chasing and imprisoning drug addicts, the amount of energy devoted to investigating and punishing corporate crime is trivial. The minimal law enforcement effort devoted to corporate criminality is almost exclusively the domain of the U.S. Department of Justice. Even with a minimum of effort, however, the discovery of widespread corporate criminality is ubiquitous, and the harms perpetrated are staggering..

The President's Commission on Organized Crime reported an ongoing investigation into money-laundering called Operation Greenback. The commission noted that there were Greenback investigations in thirty-five U.S. cities, where there were "164 arrests, 63 convictions, $38.5 million in seized currency, $7.5 million in seized property, and $117 million in IRS jeopardy and termination assessments."[61] How many burglaries, drug deals, and robberies would it take to account for that level of economic crime? Far more than ever occur.

The first major prosecution for money-laundering was that of the Great American Bank in Miami. A federal grand jury indicted the Great American Bank, charging that it laundered more than $94 million. All of the defendants in the case pleaded guilty.

In early 1986 the Treasury Department imposed a record $4.75 million civil penalty on the Bank of America for failing to report more than 17,000 large cash deposits or transfers from 1980 to 1985. In 1985 the Bank of Boston admitted to laundering $1.5 billion, Crocker National Bank $3.9 billion. For these crimes the Bank of Boston was fined $500,000; Crocker National Bank was fined $2.25 million, less than the 10 percent commission they received from the money-laundering operations. This is akin to fining a burglar $1,000 for stealing a house full of electronic equipment worth $10,000.

One of the most costly failures in U.S. economic history occurred when savings-and-loan companies began dropping like flies in the 1980s. The cost to U.S. taxpayers exceeded $500 billion as the federal government bailed out these institutions.[62] At the heart of the collapse was a system rotten to the core: "The savings and loan debacle involved a series of white-collar crimes unparalleled in American history. . . . Deliberate insider fraud was at the very center of the disaster . . . [and] systematic political collusion—not just policy error—was a critical ingredient in this unprecedented series of frauds."[63]

Robert Sherrill investigated "A Year in Corporate Crime" by analyzing the cases reported in the *Wall Street Journal*, which, as Ralph Nader pointed out, "has so much information on corporate crime it should be named 'The Crime Street Journal.'"[64] Sherrill found the following crimes reported in the *Wall Street Journal*, some of which were reported also on the business pages of America's daily press; but none received the same coverage that would be given to the arrest of a Latino gang member in South-Central Los Angeles.

Archer Daniel Midlands, "Food Basket to the World," was fined $100 million for conspiring to fix prices for two products. The profits from price fixing on only one of the products (lysine) were estimated at $170 million. Two of the officials found guilty in the price-fixing scandal were fined $350,000 and sentenced to two years in prison. The case is on appeal. The average price-fixing sentence in the 1990s was ten months. It is likely that their sentences will be reduced, as is usually the case in corporate crime cases.

General Motors was ordered by a jury in Los Angeles to pay $4.9 billion to six people who were burned when their 1979 Chevrolet Malibu exploded after its fuel tank was ruptured in a rear-end crash. Attorneys for the plaintiffs presented evidence that General Motors balked at redesigning fuel systems that they knew were dangerous because it would add $8.59 to the cost of producing the car.[65]

Shell Oil Company was fined $1.5 million in 1998 for polluting the Mississippi River, in 1997 Smithfield Foods, Inc. was fined $20 million for routinely flouting clean-water laws by dumping hog waste into a Chesapeake Bay tributary, and Koch Industries, one of the country's largest oil pipeline operators, was fined $35 million for leaking 3 million gallons of oil into lakes and steams in six states. There is no way to estimate the deaths and illnesses caused by illegal dumping of toxic wastes and other acts of pollution by corporations, but violations are rampant and enforcement lax: "The inspector general of the Environmental Protection Agency has documented widespread failures by federal and local officials to police even the most basic requirements of the nation's clean-air and clean-water laws."[66]

The worst corporate crimes are those that jeopardize the lives of workers. Failure to adhere to health and safety regulations in the workplace costs hundreds of thousands of lives. The death rate for coal miners in the United States is four to five times as high as comparable rates for European countries.[67]

In 1989 methane gas in a mine operated by the Pyro Mining Company exploded and killed ten men. The company admitted it had lied to federal investigators about the existence of hazardous conditions.

General Electric, one of the country's largest and most profitable companies, has habitually violated innumerable laws for over forty years. In the 1950s GE was fined for fixing prices on everything form small nuts and bolts to large generators sold to the government. From 1986 to 1990 GE was found guilty or pleaded no contest and (1) paid a $16.1 million fine for cheating the army on a $254 million; (2) paid a fine of $3.5 million for altering daily labor vouchers to inflate its Pentagon billings on jet engines; (3) paid a $92 million fine for attempting to bribe a Puerto Rican official; (3) paid $1 million in fines for defrauding the Air Force on a Minuteman intercontinental missile contract; (4) agreed to a sealed settlement for selling nuclear reactor parts known to be defective; (5) paid $32 million in settlements for discriminating against women and minorities; (6) paid $900,00 for overcharging the army for battle tank parts; (7) has been found responsible for no fewer than forty-seven of the Environmental Protection Agency's Superfund toxic cleanup sites; and (8) allegedly intentionally deceived consumers into buying new dishwashers by falsely saying defective appliances could not be repaired.[68]

Medical fraud is rampant. The New York University Medical Center was fined $15.5 million for submitting false financial information to the federal government regarding costs associated with research grants; Metropolitan Life Insurance was fined $20 million and agreed to pay as much as $1.7 billion to settle lawsuits by policy holders who claimed they were tricked into buying policies that ended up costing them far more than they were told the policies would cost; two top executives of one of the nation's largest health care corporations (Columbia/HCA Healthcare Corp.) resigned after the company paid $350 million in fines for defrauding the U.S. government; National Medical Care Inc. paid a $500 million fine ($101 million in criminal penalties) for charging Medicare for hundreds of thousands of needless tests for patients suffering from renal diseases; Smith-Kline Beecham's clinical laboratory agreed to pay a fine of more than $300 million for bilking Medicare for unneeded blood tests. Corning, Inc., paid $6.8 million for charging Medicare for blood tests that were never requested by doctors.

In 1997 there were over 1,000 investigations into health care fraud costing taxpayers an estimated $100 billion a year. When it comes to the nation's health, there is no limit to the fraud and corruption companies will go to for profits. Fraud in military contracts is infamous. United Telecontrol Electronics knowingly used defective bolts to attach missile launchers to airplane wings. For defrauding the Pentagon and putting lives at risk, a vice president was fined $40,000.

A kid selling ten dollars of crack would inform on this friends for such understanding.

IBM paid an $8.5 million fine for illegally selling computers to a Russian nuclear weapons laboratory.

Money-laundering has become one of the nation's major industries, involving leading banks, brokerage houses, gambling casinos, and retail businesses. Two executives of the Bank of New York admitted to laundering more than $7 billion for Russian organized crime and others seeking to avoid paying taxes and customs duties. Citibank in New York allegedly served as a conduit for laundering millions of dollars for the brother of the president of Mexico. Stock brokerage firms have been accused of laundering money from international narcotics smuggling operations. Offshore banks survive and thrive by laundering money for organized crime as well as ordinary citizens and corporations seeking to avoid paying taxes.

This list of corporate crimes could be expanded indefinitely. Were the FBI to publish a Uniform Crime Report of corporate crime, it would make the annual report of so-called Type-I offenses pale in comparison. Yet the law enforcement effort given to corporate crime is not one-tenth the effort focusing on lower-class crimes. Furthermore, as Sherrill points out: "The kindly manner in which most erring business chieftains were treated solidly underscores the fact that in the United States a prison sentence is rarely looked upon as the proper fate of corporate villains."[69] We reserve our prisons and our law enforcement efforts for the poor.

Discussion

Street crimes are a smoke screen behind which far more deadly, costly, and serious crimes take place. By any measure of harm, the crimes of police, politicians, the state, and corporations make the ordinary crimes of the poor pale by comparison. In addition to the economic and physical harms wrought by these largely unseen offenses, there is a hefty price to pay: undermining of the legitimacy of the system.

In the modern world the law is the cornerstone upon which the legitimacy of government depends. Based on this claim to legitimacy, the state maintains exclusive rights to the use of violence and guarantees universal principles of due process of law and justice.[70] When a government fails to live up to these lofty ideals, it loses legitimacy and the support of at least some parts of its citizenry. Lacking the support of its citizens, governance comes to depend on oppression and the selective application of justice. To the degree that a nation's population sees the government as defined by injustice and oppression, the government has failed. In the United States today a substantial minority of the population views the criminal law in general and the police in particular as behaving arbitrarily and as representing a corrupt, oppressive, and illegitimate force.

The reasons for the perception of the government as corrupt, oppressive, and illegitimate are not hard to find. Law enforcement agencies *do* discriminate against the poor, especially poor minorities, all the while perpetuating the myth that the poor minority population is a "dangerous class." Politicians play upon the fears of the public created by the propaganda campaigns of the law enforcement agencies themselves and promise more police, harsher laws, and more severe punishment. A vicious cycle is thereby created that becomes a self-fulfilling prophesy.

To break the cycle requires nothing less than reconstructing the role of law enforcement agencies from the way crime statistics are reported to how local law enforcement agencies are organized. The collection and reporting of data on crime must be removed from the agencies that benefit from showing crime increasing or decreasing. On the local level, independent data-gathering agencies must replace local police departments. On the federal level, as the Wickersham Commission recommended in 1931, a separate agency must be established to collect and analyze crime data and remove these responsibilities from the FBI and the Department of Justice.

It will take political leadership, which has been sorely lacking for decades, to change the public's attitude toward crime, but the task may be less onerous than one might think. It was, after all, at the height of the civil rights movement and its attendant social conflicts that Lyndon Johnson was elected president by calling for more jobs and better education for the poor as a solution to the crime problem. An equally courageous president today would begin by decriminalizing drugs and shifting the billions of dollars devoted to the so-called War on Drugs to clinics for drug addicts and improving education programs.

Organizationally, law enforcement agencies must be transformed from organizations that focus exclusively on crime control to organizations whose mission is to see that social justice, in the broadest sense of this term, is done. The process could begin by rewarding those officers who are able to resolve disputes without making an arrest rather than rewarding officers who make the most arrests.

We are at a crisis in law enforcement in America. Nothing less than fundamental changes in the laws and the legal system will solve the crisis. Failing to address this crisis will only drive us into ever-deeper divisions until we reach a point where it is too late to turn back.

Notes

1. Stuart Hall et al., *Policing the Crisis* (New York: Holmes and Meier, 1978).

2. Lincoln Steffens, *Shame of the Cities* (New York: Hill and Wang, 1957 [orig. publ. 1903]).

3. Ted Rohrlich, "Scandal Shows Why Innocent Plead Guilty," Los Angeles Times, December 31, 1999, A1.

4. Ruben Castenada and James Stockwell, "Pr. George's Hit with $4 Million Brutality Award," *Washington Post*, April 5, 2000, A1, A10.

5. Michael Kramer, "How Cops Go Bad: Brutality, Racism, Cover-ups, Lies: A Guilty Police Officer Tells How the Process Works," Time, December 15, 1997, 79–83.

6. Ibid, p. 81.

7. Alexander Cockburn, "Crazed Cops, 'Fallen Heroes,'" *The Nation*, February 14, 2000, 8.

8. Human Rights Watch, *Shielded From Justice: Police Brutality and Accountability in the United States* (New York: Human Rights Watch, 1998).

9. Wickersham Commission, *Report on Criminal Statistics* (Wahington, D.C.: GPO, 1931). William Westley in 1953 found that "brutality and the third degree have been identified with the municipal police in the United States since their inauguration in 1844." William Westley, "Violence and the Police," *American Journal of Sociology* 59 (July 1953): 34–41; Jerome H. Skolnick and James J. Fyfe, *Above the Law: Police and the Excessive Use of Force* (New York: Free Press, 1993).

10. Kramer, "How Cops Go Bad," 33.

11. U.S. Department of Justice, Federal Bureau of Investigation, FBI National Press Conference (Washington, D.C., January 21, 1998).

12. William J. Chambliss, *On The Take: From Petty Crooks to Presidents* (Bloomington: Indiana University Press, 1988). Among the hundreds of exposés of police corruption, one of the more readable ones is R. Daley, *Prince of the City: The True Story of a Cop Who Knew Too Much* (Boston: Houghton Mifflin, 1978).

13. K. Harrison, "12 on D.C. Force Arrested in Corruption Probe," *Washington Post*, December 15, 1993, A1.

14. Malcolm Gladwell, "In Drug War, Crime Sometimes Wears a Badge," *Washington Post*, May 19, 1994, A1, A16.

15. "Judge Is First Federal Jurist Convicted of Taking Bribe," *Los Angeles Times*, June 30, 1992, A4.

16. *Washington Post*, January 6, 1994, A8

17. M. Woodwiss, *Crime, Crusades, and Corruption: Prohibitions in the U.S., 1900–1987* (Totowa, N.J.: Barnes and Nobles Books Imports, 1988).

18. *Washington Post*, August 6, 1998, A1.

19. Randy Fitzgerald, "Guilty Until Proven Innocent," *Reader's Digest*, March 1, 2000, 35.

20. U.S. Department of Justice, *Annual Report of the Attorney General of the United States* [for years 1995–1997] (Washington, D.C.: Office of the Attorney General, 1995–1997).

21. "President Nixon on . . . a Political Shakedown," *Washington Post*, October 30, 1997, A19

22. Thomas B. Edsall, "GOP Angers Big Business on Key Issues: China Stance, Export Curbs Harm Trade, Groups Say," *Washington Post*, June 11, 1998, A19.

23. Alfred W. McCoy, *The Politics of Heroin in Southeast Asia* (New York: Harper and Row, 1971; William J. Chambliss, "State Organized Crime," *Criminology* 27, no. 2 (May 1989): 215–230; Jacqueline Sharkey, "The Contra-Drug Trade-off," *Common Cause* (September-October 1988): 23–33; Leslie Cockburn, *Out of Control* (New York: Atlantic Monthly Press, 1987); Jonathan Kwitny, *The Crimes of Patriots* (New York: W.W. Norton, 1987).

24. Chambliss, *On the Take*, 192.

25. Alan A. Block, "All Your Friends Are False, All Your Enemies Are Real: The CIA's Affinity for Organized Criminal Behavior," in Colin Sumner, ed., *The Blackwell Handbook of Criminology* (forthcoming).

26. Alfred W. McCoy, "The CIA Connection," *The Progressive* (July 1991): 20–26.

27. Ibid.

28. *Washington Post*, January 20, 1987, 12.

29. *The Guardian*, April 15, 1987, 30.3.

30. Michael D. Lymal and Gary Potter, *Organized Crime* (Westwood, N.J.: Prentice Hall, 1987, 2).

31. *The Guardian*, March 20, 1988, 3.

32. Alexander Cockburn and Jeffrey St. Clair, *White Out: The CIA, Drugs, and the Press* (New York: Verso, 1998), 264.

33. Hearings Before the Senate Select Committee on Assassinations, 94th Cong., 1st Sess., November 20 (Washington, D.C.: GPO, 1986).

34. *The Guardian*, December 31, 1986, R–16.2, 3.

35. *The Guardian*, July 29, 1987, R–41.1, 2.

36. *Washington Post*, December 14, 1986.

37. Ibid.

38. Jim Hougan, *Spooks: The Haunting of America* (New York: William Morrow, 1978), 204–207)

39. Senate Select Committee, 1975

40. Ibid.

41. *New York Times*, May 13, 1985, R1.

42. *The Nation*, January 8, 1987, 92

43. Gary Potter and Bruce Bullington, "Drug Trafficking and the Contras," paper delivered at the American Society of Criminology, Montreal, 1987,38.

44. Hougan, *Spooks*, 123–138.

45. Ibid., 132.

46. *New York Times*, December 16, 1986, 18.

47. Potter and Bullington, "Drug Trafficking and the Contras," 4.

48. *The Guardian*, April 15, 1987, R30.

49. John Dinges and Saul Landau, *Assassination on Embassy Row* (New York: McGraw Hill, 1980), 239.

50. Penny Lernoux, "The Miami Connection," *The Nation*, February 18, 1984, 186–198.

51. Ibid., 188.

52. *The Guardian*, January 16, 1985, 6.

53. United States Commission on CIA Activities within the United States. *Report to the President* (the Rockefeller Report) (Washington, D.C.: GPO, 1975).

54. Ibid., 101-115

55. Jack Anderson and Lee Whitten, "The CIA's Sex Squad," *Washington Post*, September 5, 1977, 1; John Jacobs, "The Diaries of a CIA Operative," *Washington Post*, August 1, 1977, 1; John M. Crewdson and J. Thomas, "Abuses in Testing of Drugs by CIA to Be Panel Focus," *New York Times*, September 20, 1977, 1.

56. Noam Chomsky, *The Chomsky Trilogy: Secrets, Lies, and Democracy* (Boston: Odonian Press, 1988).

57. General Accounting Office, *The CIA and the Office of Public Diplomacy*, report to Congress (Washington, D.C.: GPO, 1987), 54.

58. James William Coleman, *The Criminal Elite* (New York: St. Martin's Press, 1996), 7

59. Kitty Calavita, Henry N. Pontell, and Robert H. Tillman, *Big Money Crime: Fraud and Politics in the Savings and Loan Crisis* (Berkeley, University of California Press, 1997).

60. Judy Root Aulette and Raymond Michalowski, "Fire in Hamlet: A Case Study of a State-Corporate Crime," in Kenneth D. Tunnell (ed.), *Political Crime in Contemporary America: A Critical Approach* (New York: Garland Publishing, 1993), 171.

61. Nathaniel Nash, "Bank of America Is Told to Pay U.S. $4.75 Million Fine," *New York Times*, January 22, 1986, A1, D5.

62. Calavita, et al., *Big Money Crime.*

63. Ibid., 1.

64. Robert Sherrill, "A Year in Corporate Crime," *The Nation*, April 7, 1997, 11–24.

65. Jeffrey Ball and Milo Geyelin, "GM Ordered by Jury to Pay $4.9 Billion," *Wall Street Journal*, July 12, 1999, A3.

66. John H. Cushman Jr., "EPA Audits Find the Dirty Truth," *Denver Post*, June 5, 1998, 1A.

67. Daniel Curran, *Dead Laws for Dead Men* (Pittsburgh: University of Pittsburgh Press, 1993).

68. William Greider, *Who Will Tell the People* (1992); Carolyn Mayer, "Dispute Escalates in GE Dishwasher Recall," *Washington Post*, Feb. 19, 2000, A4.

69. Sherrill, "A Year in Corporate Crime," 24.

70. William J. Chambliss and Robert B. Seidman, *Law, Order, and Power* (Reading, Mass.: Addison-Wesley, 1982).

Chapter Eight

Summary, Conclusions, and Solutions

For the past thirty-five years conservative Republicans and (mostly southern) Democrats, in league with law enforcement agencies and the equally conservative media, have succeeded in convincing the U.S. public that we are facing a "crime problem" of unprecedented dimensions. Buttressing the rhetoric of politicians and the alarmism of the media, law enforcement agencies have manipulated statistics and distorted reality.

The Republican party's "Southern Strategy," designed to elect Barry Goldwater in 1964, Richard Nixon in 1968, Ronald Reagan in 1980, and George Bush in 1988, succeeded for all but Goldwater. So successful was the strategy that the Democrats co-opted it and made fighting crime a cornerstone of the Clinton-Gore campaigns.

With the exception of Jimmy Carter, every president since Lyndon Johnson has equated crime with lower-class African Americans. They have become America's modern-day "dangerous class," portrayed as a culture of "welfare queens" breeding criminal children living in a war zone of drugs and guns.

Law enforcement agencies have seized the opportunity to ensure their own organizational interests and policies. Crime data are manipulated and the news media are fed distorted pictures about crime waves, gangs, drugs, drive-by shootings, and a host of other horrific problems. Law enforcement efforts focus on policing the ghetto. The crimes of law enforcement agencies, governments, politicians, and corporations are ignored or relegated to the business pages of the newspaper. Thus is the crime control industry assured a constant increase in money and power.

Like all successful bureaucracies, law enforcement agencies—from the U.S. Department of Justice to rural sheriff's offices—enforce the laws in ways that minimize strain and maximize rewards for the organization. In the day-to-day practice of law enforcement agencies, this translates into enforcing the laws that are violated by the lower classes, minimally enforcing the laws violated by the middle and upper classes, and selectively enforcing the laws that are violated by all social classes—such as using illegal drugs or driving under the influence of alcohol—against the lower classes or treating the transgressions of the middle and upper classes leniently.

The practices and patterns of the politicians, media, and law enforcement agencies hide the corruption and criminality of government, corporations, and law enforcement officials.

Dire consequences follow from these institutionalized patterns of creating myths about crime, defining lower-class minorities as inherently criminal, and selectively enforcing criminal laws. The minorities who experience the sting of the law are alienated from society and see the law not as a source of protection but as a mechanism of oppression. The middle classes grow cynical about the government, to the point that criminality, corruption, and malfeasance are not grounds for impeachment or censure but, rather, expected behavior that can be overlooked so long as the stock market is sound and the unemployment rate low. The legitimacy of officeholders no longer depends on upholding principles of fairness and social justice; it depends solely on the ability to use power for personal and political gain.

Solutions are not hard to find, but they are difficult to implement for they fly in the face of conventional wisdom and the interests of powerful institutions. It is a lead-pipe cinch that politicians will continue to use crime as a political football whenever convenient. Law enforcement agencies will continue to distort and lie about crime rates to meet their particular needs at any point in time. The crime control industry will continue to lobby and propagandize to buttress their profits and increase the size of their bureaucracies. The opponents of reform are numerous and powerful. Nonetheless, some solutions are possible that could make a real difference.

1. The movement toward more-severe sentences for all offenders, juveniles and adults alike, must be reversed. Drugs must be decriminalized. Minor offenders, whatever their class or color, should be treated with kid gloves, not an iron fist. A prerequisite for all of this is the creation of an honest and scientifically reliable system for recording and describing the extent and seriousness of crime.
2. Because politicians will use whatever means they can to gain political advantage over their opponents, a well-informed press must be skeptical of reports from politicians and law enforcement agencies about crime trends, and must inform the public of misleading information. Training journalists in the use and misuse of statistics and their sources could considerably reduce the ability of politicians and the law enforcement bureaucracy to distort the facts.
3. The responsibility for collecting and reporting crime statistics and for determining research agendas must be removed from the crime control agencies that have a vested interest in the outcomes of the reports and the research. A separate federal agency, modeled after the Census Bureau, must be established to coordinate the gathering and reporting of data and the allocation of money for research on crime.
4. All of the law enforcement bureaucracies must be put under civilian control. Civilian review boards that emerged in the 1960s to rein in the excesses of local police have never been given either sufficient authority or the financial resources to do their job. They lack independent investigative resources, and their findings go unpublicized. The obstacles that police put in the way of civilian review boards make them largely ineffective. Creating institutions that will serve to "guard the guardians" is crucial to making law enforcement compatible with democracy.
5. The training of police officers must be reoriented at all levels away from the military model, which perpetuates a culture of violence and a war zone mentality. The emphasis on the

use of force should be replaced with an emphasis on conflict resolution.

6. Within the organization of policing, the reward system must be turned upside down. Officers should be recognized and promoted not on the basis of the number of arrests they make but on their ability to work as a team to control crime and settle conflicts without invoking the criminal justice system.
7. Prosecutors must be trained in forms of conflict and dispute resolution that stress alternatives to prosecution and incarceration. And the office of prosecutor must be depoliticized. So long as prosecutors' aspirations for reelection, lucrative private sector employment, or higher political office depends on their track record of convictions and prison sentences, vulnerable and defenseless suspects will continue to flood the justice system and prisons. Prosecutors should be appointed and the quality of their performance judged by their ability to resolve disputes without criminal sanctions.
8. Institutions must be created that will "guard the guardians." For years police review boards have fumbled along with little power and less effect. Despite millions of dollars in claims paid to citizens abused by police and endless exposés of law enforcement corruption, the system remains unchanged. We must create mechanisms for ferreting out the misfeasance and malfeasance of law enforcement agencies. This can only be accomplished by independent agencies empowered to force organizational and structural changes.
9. The problem of corporate crimes must be addressed. As a very minimal beginning, extant laws must be enforced. The savings realized from releasing minor offenders, from the decriminalization of drug laws, and from the redeployment of police into the community will generate more than enough money to fund the enforcement of laws against corporations.

These are modest proposals. But even modest proposals require great leadership in a world where bureaucracies resist change.

The ideal of a legal system that promises justice for all is one of the loftiest ever planted in the soil of human society. When the law favors the rich and punishes the poor the ideal is destroyed. Failing to achieve that lofty ideal, or worse, making a mockery of it in the day-to-day operations of the criminal justice system, divides a country and undermines the very stability the law was designed to accomplish. FBI Director Louis Freeh was speaking of police corruption but he could well have been addressing the entire issue of the structural biases built into law enforcement in the United States when he observed, "The insidious nature of police corruption inherently undermines the confidence of the American people in one of the basic tenets of democracy—that law enforcement officers will honestly and fairly protect and serve the citizens to whom they answer."[1] Law enforcement in the United States fails to "honestly and fairly protect and serve [all] the citizens." Nothing short of fundamental changes in the way crime is perceived and criminal law is enforced will suffice. Such changes can and must be achieved if we are to bring the lofty idea of "justice for all" to reality.

Note

1. Federal Bureau of Investigation, "Police Corruption" (Washington, D.C.: FBI National Press Office, January 21, 1998), 1.

Index